EQUITY INCOME ANALYTICS

Dedicated to my family

TABLE OF CONTENTS

INTRODUCTION

Dividends and dividend growth are regarded as essential elements of retirement investing. Rankings for dividend-paying and dividend growth stocks have been developed to aid investors in stock selection. (Note 1) Moreover, given trends in longevity, retirements can reach up to 30 years or more, during which even moderate-to-low inflation can erode purchasing power.

Accordingly, a better understanding of the ability of firms to pay and grow dividends may be of increasing relevance to retirees as well as investors saving for retirement. This book is a preliminary effort to (1) document a basic analytical framework to evaluate a firm's capacity to generate an income for equity investors, and (2) to present results based on the framework for firms grouped by sector and subsector. The data and information contained herein are subject to revisions, and shortcomings of the research are noted. The book is divided into two major sections, the analytical framework, and results of the analysis. The results are presented in reports employing data from non-financial firms worldwide with total market capitalization of approximately US$ 3.8 trillion as of 2014.

PART I. ANALYTICAL FRAMEWORK

DEFINITIONS AND CLARIFICATIONS

The *total* return of an equity investment is generally said to be comprised of two types of return: *Income*, typically from cash dividends or distributions, and *capital appreciation*, from the appreciated value of the stock. (Note 2)

The aim of equity income analytics is to evaluate a firm's capacity to generate income for equity investors. (Note 3) This capacity is assumed to exist regardless of whether or not dividends are paid; therefore the analysis can be applied to both dividend-paying and non-dividend paying firms; if no dividend is paid the equity income could be thought of as *potential*. Reference to dividends generally means *cash* dividends or cash distributions unless otherwise indicated.

Equity Income Generating Capacity

It is assumed that the capacity of a firm to generate equity income for investors relies on at least three key elements:

Identifying the Primary Source of Equity Income. The income for equity investors is assumed to originate from the firm's *internal, essential and recurring operations*, and can be referred to as the *primary source of equity income*. Because equity income is ultimately realized in the form of cash dividends or distributions, the term *primary source of payment* is also used in the context of *payment*. The next section will be devoted to establishing a best approximation of this primary source, as there are many possible measures.

Sufficient Coverage. The primary source of payment must be sufficient to cover any cash dividends, whether or not currently paid.

Sustainability. The primary source of payment must be *consistently* able to cover dividends. This requires that the source of payment be recurring, although significant variability may be expected in the natural course of business.

Alternative (secondary, tertiary) sources of payment are not viewed as contributing to capacity, as they have an external, non-operating source of cash flow, as described in the section on alternative sources of repayment.

Primary Source of Equity Income

Identifying the most appropriate primary source of equity income is a foundation for evaluating the capacity of the firm to generate equity income for investors.

However, when translated into financial terminology, the primary source may not be entirely clear. Analysts appear to be divided in the use of accrual-based and cash flow measures. Moreover, the term "cash flow" can be defined in a number of ways, not all of which can reasonably considered to be a primary source of equity income when examined more closely; various approaches to defining cash flow should be sorted through and classified.

To begin, a distinction is drawn between two common terms, *accrual earnings* and *cash flow* (cash flow also can include *accrual earnings-based* cash flow). Clarifications will be provided below. (Note 4)

Accrual Earnings. Examples of accrual earnings are covered here. In accounting, since retained earnings are increased by increases in net earnings, and dividends are paid out of retained earnings (debit to retained earnings and credit to cash), net earnings may be viewed as a source of payment for dividends. In finance, the *residual-dividend model* is generally assumed to pay out dividends from accrual earnings; these *residual earnings* refer to the earnings that do not need to be reinvested into the business in order to maintain the company's target capital structure.

Shim, Siegel and Dauber use accrual earnings in the definition of dividend-paying capacity as follows: *Earnings x Dividend payout percentage*. (2008: 61.14) The term dividend-paying capacity, which is found in the context of specialized valuation analysis, might be more closely described as a *source of payment* for dividends.

Shim and Siegel (2007) also state that for the purpose of forecasting cash flows many analysts prefer current accrual accounting earnings (2007: 440).

Cash Flow

The term "cash flow" can give rise to considerable confusion as well as error. Two types of "cash flow" can be identified: The first type of cash flow measure *is accrual earnings-based* and is considered to be an incomplete source of payment. The second type centers on the concept of *free cash flow*, and is considered to be a reasonable approximation to a source of payment for dividends. Each type is described below.

Cash Flow (Accrual Earnings-Based). The following measures of what is often referred to as "cash flow" are considered inadequate because they ignore essential cash (out)flows, in particular *capital expenditures* (abbreviated *capex*) and *changes in working capital*. Their formulas are based on accrual earnings figures, with certain non-cash items added back, as follows: (*Net income + depreciation)* or (*Net income + depreciation + amortization)*. This definition may also sometimes be called *funds flow*. Another measure of cash flow, EBITDA, is earnings before interest, taxes, depreciation and amortization.

It could be argued that depreciation is a reasonable approximation for capex, and therefore can be used in its place. However there is evidence that the amount of depreciation can fall short of the actual capital investments required and therefore cannot necessarily be assumed to be cash flow available to cover debt service. In a sample of 51 firms that had defaulted on their debt, 69% of the companies had invested *more* than their depreciation amounts and the EBITDA measure overestimated cash flow interest coverage prior to default. (Moody's 2000: 4) While EBITDA *less capex* could be used to correct for the overstated cash flow, changes in working capital remain unaccounted for.

Cash Flow--Best Approximation. The following examples are measures of cash flow that are considered to best approximate a primary source of equity income and payment for dividends: NCF and FCF; both of these measures account for capital expenditures and both capital expenditures and changes in working capital.

NCF. Hitchner (2011) uses the term *net cash flow* or *net free cash flow* (both abbreviated as NCF). (Note 5) The formula for NCF is Earnings before interest and taxes – taxes on EBIT at effective tax rate + depreciation – capital expenditures plus/minus changes in working capital. (2011:500)

FCF. The corporate finance literature also uses *free cash flow* (FCF) in security valuation. Rosenbaum and Pearl (2013) compute free cash flow starting with earnings before interest and after taxes (EBIAT). Their formula for FCF is:

FCF=EBIAT + Depreciation and Amortization - Capex - increase/ (decrease) in net working capital (2013: 131, 163).

Because of their similarity, NCF and FCF may often be used interchangeably.

It is recognized that NCF is not a measure in accordance with Generally Accepted Accounting Principles (GAAP).

In addition to the computations for NCF (or FCF) above, an alternative measure of NCF can be obtained by referring to a company's financial statements as follows: *Net cash from operations* (NCO) from the cash flow statement of a company's financial statements, less capital expenditures (also from the cash flow statement, in the Investing section). NCO may roughly correspond to the formula above for NCF and FCF after adjusting for changes in net working capital but *before* deducting capex.

The preferred term for cash flow as the primary source of equity income and payment for dividends is *net free cash flow* or *net cash flow* (NCF), in accordance with Hitchner (2011). NCF can be defined as the net cash flow from the recurring, essential operations of the business, less capital (and other) expenditures required for the business to remain competitive in its industry.

NCF might be viewed as a form of net profitability *in a cash flow sense*, but the section on possible extensions to the analysis should be consulted for the discussion on a modified NCF.

An interesting question is whether cash flow or accrual earnings are of more relevance to firms in their actual payment of dividends. Brigham and Houston (2004) cite the case of Chevron-Texaco corporation in which a greater correlation was found between dividends and cash flows than between dividends and earnings; payout ratios also appear to have more closely tracked cash flows than earnings (2004: 535-536).

Multiple Purposes for NCF. It should be emphasized that NCF is also the source of payment for other non-operating purposes of the business including *debt service*, share repurchases, the build-up of cash reserves or investments in various short-term financial instruments for non-operating purposes. (Note 6)

Alternative Sources of Payment

If the primary source of payment is insufficient to cover dividend payments, it could be argued that secondary (or tertiary) sources of payment can be drawn upon to cover the shortfall; this could include liquidation of short-term investments, non-essential assets or the issuance of equity. In a low-interest rate environment, cheap borrowings to finance dividends may be appealing. However, these alternatives may not be without consequences for the firm, and they do not replace NCF as the primary source of payment for dividends. (Note 7)

EVALUATING CAPACITY

Having settled on NCF as a reasonable approximation of the primary source of equity income, financial ratios can be used to evaluate the capacity for equity income generation. The capacity ratios examined are Dividend Coverage, the NCF Ratio, NCO/Revenues and Capex/Revenues ratio.

Dividend Coverage. In ratio analysis both accrual earnings and cash flow measures are used in the numerator for the calculation of the *dividend coverage ratio*, a financial metric used to gauge the ability of the firm to cover its dividend payments. For the following hypothetical data for a given fiscal year: NCF=40, cash dividends paid=20, the dividend coverage ratio is simply calculated as NCF/ Cash Dividends or 40/20= 2.0.

For firms that do not pay a dividend, it may be possible to compute a hypothetical dividend amount based on a target coverage ratio.

An alternative version of a dividend coverage ratio incorporating *debt service* is also presented in the section on possible extensions to the analysis.

Deteriorating Trends and the NCF Ratio. It may not possible to draw a conclusion regarding the desirability of revenue growth without consideration of the net cash flow (NCF) generated out of those revenues.

Each case would need to be examined separately, but a case which could be overlooked is one in which dividend coverage appears to be improving due to rising NCF in *absolute* terms. However, NCF relative to revenues may provide a better basis for evaluation: NCF rising more slowly than revenues may signal a secular weakening in the firm's capacity to support dividend payments. A simple yet fundamental metric using the primary source of equity income in the numerator and revenues in the denominator can be applied to capture such a relative deterioration: *Net free cash flow/Revenues* (NCF/Revs). This ratio can be referred to as the *NCF Ratio* (or *FCF ratio* if the term *free cash flow* is preferred). From the example above, if revenues for the year were 400, the NCF ratio would be calculated as 40/ 400 = 0.10

Another case is that of *declining* revenues associated with a rising NCF relative to revenues. While revenue declines may generally be viewed negatively, there may be less cause for concern if the smaller revenues are generating increasing net cash flow relative to revenues over the long-term and the dividend coverage remains adequate or is improving.

Historical Data. Identification of deteriorating fundamentals may require more historical data; a minimum of three to five years may be acceptable, but if data are obtainable, as many as ten years is preferable; it is acknowledged that even then the sample size remains small.

So-called accounting trickery can occur and may be difficult to detect over short periods, particular with a single year of data. However, over longer periods of time, a truer picture of the company's financial condition may emerge.

Additional historical data can not only help identify the development of a long-term trend, but aids in comparisons between long-term trends and recent performance. For example, a decline in the NCF/Revenue ratio over a 7-year period from, say, 0.25 to 0.10, could be indicative of a secular weakening capacity to generate an income for equity investors. Another important point concerns capital expenditures, which can in some industries can vary significantly from year to year and an overall pattern may not be identifiable over the short-term.

Causal Factors and Economic Theory

Should a declining trend in the *NCF/revenues* ratio be observed, two main component measures of NCF, net cash from operations (NCO), and capital expenditures (Capex), and their relationship to revenues over time *NCO/Revs* and *Capex/Revs* may offer additional insight. Does impaired capacity originate from poor management or from the broader economic environment (or a combination of both)? Economic theory may help provide some clarity.

Certain external forces such as monetary policy may be more difficult for individual managers to control and can have both beneficial and negative influences on the firm. For example, a policy of lowering interest rates can stimulate additional activity that would otherwise not have occurred and set into motion a variety of events.

Consumer Goods. Consumers may benefit from lowered interest rates, both in the form of cheaper borrowing costs to finance the purchase of consumer goods, but also in the form of savings on existing debt service obligations such as mortgage payments (assuming refinancing at a lower interest rate). The savings can increase disposable income and spur purchases that otherwise would not have been made in the absence of the lowered interest rates.

Firms may benefit from the policy, at least temporarily, from a boost in their revenues and net cash flow from operations (NCO). It is also possible that the policy may push up consumer goods prices somewhat to induce firms to supply the additional volume of purchases.

In a rising interest-rate environment, the reverse may occur, leading to falling revenues and NCO.

NCO. It is expected that astute managers can find ways to improve NCO by controlling expenses and managing operating assets more efficiently such as through improved receivables or inventory turnover.

However, when the company receives a boost in revenues and NCO from expansionary monetary policy measures, managers may be pleased with the results and not perceive any underlying problem associated with this external factor. Unfortunately, in the opposite case of a contractionary policy environment, layoffs and other cost-control measures may need to be implemented with a severity that would not have otherwise occurred.

Capex and Capital Goods Markets. Capital expenditures may present a different challenge to management. While managers may appear to be acting rationally, the external signal generated by monetary policy may bias decision-making and have long-lasting consequences for firms as described below.

As noted above, if consumer goods purchases are rising, the argument for adding more capital equipment than would have otherwise been purchased may be considered justified. Moreover, the decline in interest rates can stimulate additional borrowings by firms as the purchase of capital equipment appears more profitable. For either or both reasons, firms throughout an industry may tend to act similarly, collectively boosting their investments in capital equipment at approximately the same time, and possibly influencing an upward movement of the prices of capital goods.

A major concern is that later in the cycle, after the initial policy-induced boost of consumer goods purchases has waned, firms may suffer serious consequences. The collective overproduction of the goods produced by the overinvested capital equipment may lead to steep price declines of those goods, dissipation of profitability, possible losses and in extreme cases, default and bankruptcy. Firms that rely heavily on capital expenditures may be more adversely affected than those in other less capital-intensive industries, suffering higher capex costs relative to revenues at the outset, and bearing the brunt of greater relative consumer goods price declines towards the end.

If such policy-induced economic cycles can be said to exist, then it also may be possible to break down the phases of the cycle for an industry, whether expansionary, recessionary or relatively "stable." This also may aid in predicting periods during which industry-wide NCF might be more likely to come under pressure, and not necessarily due to normally-distributed random factors or poor management. Although beyond the scope of this discussion, because the theory of economic cycles tends to hinge on the subject of interest rates, the theory of real interest rate determination may be worth further investigation. (Note 8)

In combination with industry analysis and comparison to peers in the industry it also may be possible to pinpoint firms for poor decision-making *independent* of any economic cycles or phases. In such a case, selection of capital equipment may have been inadequate to respond to competition and the market, with possible negative consequences for the firm's long-term equity income generating capacity.

POSSIBLE EXTENSIONS TO ANALYSIS

There remain a number of shortcomings to the above analysis. The following items are proposed to fine-tune, and potentially improve upon, the analysis of equity income generating capacity.

Modified NCF.   As discussed above, capital expenditures are deducted to arrive at net free cash flow (NCF). However, capex as reported may exclude certain items. Moreover, there may be other types of investment expenditures necessary to achieve or maintain dominance in an industry. For example, if a firm tends to make recurring business acquisitions, it could be argued that in addition to capital expenditures, cash outflows for business acquisitions should also be deducted to arrive at a more accurate figure for NCF.

Acquisitions and investments can take many forms, and terminology may also vary. This could include the following examples which in some cases may represent significant amounts:
Acquisition of licenses, technology and patents
Capitalization of software costs (not included in capex)
Purchases of certain intangible assets
Acquisition of investments in consolidated undertakings
Purchases of long-term investments
Investments in non-marketable equity investments
Acquisition of interests/investments in JVs
Acquisition of investments in associates

Modified Dividend Coverage

Types of Payments. Cash dividend payments to be included in the coverage ratio should be recurring cash dividends on both ordinary and preferred shares. Other types of recurring cash distributions should be included. *Special dividends* and *liquidating dividends* could possibly be excluded from computations for *recurring* dividend payments, but should be at least noted as such. Stock dividends would also be excluded.

Dividend growth is often based on a measure of dividends *per share*. However, because firms can increase the per share growth rate by repurchasing shares, the *actual amount* of dividends, unadjusted by the number of shares outstanding, is a preferred base upon which to calculate dividend growth.

Dividend Coverage and Debt service. Since the primary source of payment for dividends, NCF, is also considered to be the primary source of repayment for debt, a more comprehensive analysis of equity income generating capacity might integrate debt service requirements.

In credit analysis, a simple metric of ability of a firm to service its debt is the *debt service coverage* (DSC) ratio. The numerator is a figure representing the source of repayment for the loan, depending on the preference of the analyst; and the denominator is the amount of debt to be serviced ("debt service") in that same period. Debt service is defined as principal plus interest (P+i). The numerator may also be a form of "stabilized" or "normalized" net income or cash flow depending on the analysis.

The dividend coverage ratio could be modified to incorporate debt service by combining dividends and debt service (P + i) in the denominator and the primary source of payment in the numerator. Such a ratio might be called a *dividend-debt service coverage ratio* (DDS coverage ratio). An example with the previous hypothetical data is as follows: NCF = 40, cash dividends paid=20, principal repayments of debt=10 and interest =5, then this modified coverage ratio could be calculated as NCF/ [(Cash Dividends) + (P+i)], or (40 / 35) = 1.14.

Non-Cash Transactions

Non-cash income potentially overstates the ability of a company to pay dividends from cash flow. Therefore, to improve the accuracy of cash flow measures, special care should be taken to identify non-cash transactions. A few examples of non-cash items that can appear to inflate cash flow include: Income/undistributed earnings according to the *equity method* of accounting for investments, gains on inventory due to increased valuation, deferred and amortized gain on sale of assets in sale-leaseback accounting, unrealized gains on marketable equity securities, and minority interest income. Financial statements that include a statement of cash flows may adjust for non-cash items (Note 9)

ADDITIONAL CONSIDERATIONS

Further study can expand upon the analytical framework. Areas for further examination are listed below.

Industry/Sector. A comprehensive analysis of equity income generating capacity includes a thorough understanding of the industry in which the firm operates as well as the application of traditional tools of financial analysis; credit analysis can be useful for companies with debt servicing requirements.

Revenues. Critical to analysis of the quality of the revenue stream is to identify whether any portion of revenues involves large related-party transactions/relationships that represent a lack of independence and control by the entity under analysis. Customer concentrations including reliance on revenue from government contracts also should be examined closely.

Capital Expenditures. A more in-depth understanding of the nature of the capital expenditures would be highly useful in evaluating firms, and especially for those that tend to be capital-intensive. Capex may often be treated as uniform with little if any distinction made between *maintenance capex* (roughly defined as a level of capex required for the business to maintain its position in the industry), and capital expenditures intended to propel the firm towards a dominant position in the industry.

Another point worth consideration is that acquisition of other investments including businesses may be viewed as a variation of capex, as both assets and technology transfer are likely integral to the acquisition. Refer back to the discussion on modified NCF in the section on possible extensions to the analysis.

Probability Theory. Estimates for the arithmetic mean of various measures are generally assumed to follow an approximately normal distribution. The central limit theorem provides a basis for the normality assumption, and roughly stated, relies upon the outcomes being generated additively and by numerous small independent processes.

A major concern is whether financial data and measures such as those presented herein tend to be influenced by a dominant external force relative to other impacts, and whether some processes may not be independent. This issue was touched upon in the context of economic theory above, where monetary policy may exert a significant impact on economic activity.

Therefore, some form of normality testing could be a useful supplementary tool of analysis. Further research is recommended on the underlying probability distributions and the economic dynamics. Accordingly, attempting forecasting and constructing forecasting models without consideration of the above could produce questionable results.

Quality of Financial Information. The quality of the source financial information can also impact upon the results of an analysis of equity income generating capacity. Even audited financial statements may include estimates which may or may not fully and accurately reflect the financial condition of the firm at all times. For smaller firms with unaudited financial statements, reliability of the financial information is a potentially major issue, and particular attention should be paid to unexplained items, including unexplained adjustments to retained earnings. Frequent changes of auditors, CPAs, or tax preparers can also be a cause for concern.

Occasional misclassification of long-term non-operating assets into operating cash flow can distort the figure upward for operating cash flow in individual years when those assets are liquidated. This problem also may relate to the quality of financial information.

Footnotes

1. Rankings are established according to the long-term dividend-paying track records of firms; ranked stocks may be popularly referred to as "dividend stalwarts," "dividend achievers," "dividend champions" and "dividend aristocrats."

2. The return from *capital appreciation* of a stock is viewed as fundamentally distinct from the return from equity *income*. Return from capital appreciation requires that in order to realize cash, the investor must either liquidate, or borrow against, the appreciated stock. This would include share repurchases in which the firm happens to purchase the stock from a shareholder. Note that funds referred to as *equity income funds* may aim for both income and capital growth.

3. Income can also be earned from investments in debt instruments such as bonds, often referred to as *fixed income*. The term *equity income* should also be distinguished from the income earned by a firm (as in "net income").

4. Clarification of terms: The terms "net profit" "net income" and "net earnings" and "earnings" can be used interchangeably, and are assumed to be accrual-based unless otherwise indicated. The term "cash flow" has numerous possible definitions as covered in the section on the primary source of equity income.

5. Two variations of NCF are proposed by Hitchner (2011): NCF to overall invested capital which is associated with both debt and equity

and is also called *invested capital net cash flow;* and NCF to equity, also referred to as *equity net cash flows.* This latter variation is referred to as dividend-paying capacity (2011:648). As noted earlier, Shim, Siegel and Dauber (2008) define dividend-paying capacity with accrual net earnings. However, regardless of the definition, dividend-paying capacity might be more closely described as a source of payment for dividends rather than as the capacity of the firm to pay dividends.

6. Debt service is defined as the return of principal and payment of interest (P+i). When referring to debt service, the term the primary source of *repayment* is used rather than primary source of payment. Debt service is also discussed in the section on possible extensions to the analysis.

7. In the field of credit analysis, a parallel can be drawn with debt service capacity. For example, if a company's primary source of *repayment* for debt becomes insufficient, from the creditor's standpoint (e.g. bank, bondholder), the risk of default on the loan can be viewed as more likely. Reliance on alternative sources of repayment such as additional debt accumulation or equity issuance may result in future burdens on the company, the investors, or result in untimely asset liquidations. Debt restructuring may eventually be necessary to better match the company cash flow to debt service requirements.

8. It could be argued that in response to an expansionary policy stimulus managers should attempt to refrain from taking advantage of lowered borrowing costs to acquire capital equipment. This may be difficult in practice. Economic cycles featuring expansionary periods and recessions may be characterized by changes in relative prices of capital and consumer goods. (Huerta de Soto 2012). Also see the discussion in the section on probability theory.

9. Other non-cash transactions include income from litigation or settlements where a receivable is generated but is non-cash until collection. Long-term debt that is converted into a *demand note,* if reclassified into short-term operating debt could inflate operating cash flow. This discussion of non-cash transactions is not comprehensive and each firm and industry may present special cases.

References

Brigham, Eugene F., and Houston, Joel F., *Fundamentals of Financial Management*, 10th Edition, South-Western, 2004.

Damodaran, Aswath., *Investment Valuation: Tools and Techniques for Determining the Value of any Asset*, 3rd Edition, Wiley Finance, 2012.

Hitchner, James R., *Financial Valuation: Applications and Models*, 3rd Edition, John Wiley & Sons, 2011

Huerta de Soto, Jesus., *Money, Bank Credit, and Economic Cycles*, Ludwig von Mises Institute 2012.

Moody's Investors Service Global Credit Research, "Putting EBITDA in Perspective," *Special Comment*, June 2000.

Rosenbaum, Joshua., Pearl, Joshua., *Investment Banking: Valuation, Leveraged Buyouts, and Mergers & Acquisitions*, (2nd Ed.), 2013.

Shim, Jae K., and Siegel, Joel., *Handbook of Financial Analysis, Forecasting, and Modeling*, 2007.

Shim, Jae K., Siegel, Joel and Dauber, Nick *Corporate Controller's Handbook of Financial Management 2008-2009* (2008).

Annual financial statements of the firms under study were sourced from the filings with the U.S. Securities and Exchange Commission (SEC) or from company annual reports containing financial statements. The NASDAQ, Wikipedia, Wikinvest and Yahoo Finance websites were consulted for financial and other information.

PART II. ANALYTICAL RESULTS

READING THE REPORTS

Each report represents an equity income analysis of a firm and begins with the subsector in which the firm is classified and the observation period.

Section Structure. There are four major sections to each report, each corresponding to the following financial metrics: Cash Dividend Growth Rate, Dividend Coverage Ratio, Net Cash Flow Ratio, and Components of NCF (which consist of NCO/Revenues and Capital expenditures/Revenues; Capital expenditures may be abbreviated by "capex").

A note preceding the charts is intended to clarify that the metrics may not be normally distributed. For more information on this topic, see the relevant comments on probability theory in the framework section.

Each section features a chart of the particular financial metric followed by estimates for the sample mean (labelled "period average") and the sample standard deviation (labelled "dispersion") for each metric over the observation period.

The charts should be fairly self-explanatory; further details about each of these metrics and their context in the analysis are covered in the framework section.

Charts may feature a simple *trend line* for rough reference purposes, but it may be of limited use.

For companies that pay no dividend for all or part of the period observed, the charts of the first two sections will be incomplete or blank. Moreover, the estimates for the average and dispersion, may also appear blank or show an error message such as (#DIV/0!).

Each of the four sections is discussed in further detail here.

1. Cash Dividend Growth Rate

Dividend growth itself is not an indicator of the firm's capacity to generate equity income, but this dividend growth measure is provided for reference purposes. The year-on-year growth rate of dividends is presented in this chart, although another useful indicator of growth, the compound annual growth rate (CAGR) is not presently shown.

Note that for an observation period of 6 years, since the year-on-year growth rate draws from the previous year, only 5 data points are available for the chart and the estimates (sample size of 5).

The dividends refer to the *actual amount* of cash dividends reported paid for each year on the financial statements and are not adjusted per share figures.

2. Dividend Coverage Ratio

The dividend coverage ratio is computed by dividing NCF (net cash flow) by the *actual amount* of cash dividends reported paid for each year as explained just above.

The dividend coverage ratio does not take into account debt service coverage. The importance of debt service and possible extension to the analysis is covered in the framework section.

3. Net Cash Flow Ratio

This metric is computed as net cash flow divided by revenues. *Net cash flow* (NCF) is also commonly referred to as *free cash flow* (FCF). NCF is generally defined as net cash from operations less capital expenditures, with possible modifications. Refer to the framework section for details.

4. Components of NCF

The chart shows two major components of NCF: Net cash from operations divided by revenues (NCO/Revs) and Capital expenditures divided by revenues (CAPEX/Revs). The figures are presented as ratios in both the chart and the estimates.

The information contained in the reports are for reference purposes and should not be taken as investment advice or as recommendations.

Summary of Sector and Subsector Groupings

For further explanations of sector and subsector data and methodology, see Appendix 1. In the summary list below, the number of firms represented in each sector is shown. Under Beverages-Production & Distribution, three subsectors are counted (Wineries & Distillers, Brewers, and Soft Drinks). Under Semiconductor, two subsectors are counted (Integrated Circuits and Broad Line).

Basic Materials Sector (3 subsectors, 5 firms)

Oil & gas production 2

Independent Oil & Gas 1

Integrated oil companies 2

Consumer Goods Sector (6 subsectors, 9 firms)

Auto manufacturing 3

Beverages-Production & Distribution:

Wineries & Distillers 1

Beverages- Brewers 1

Beverages-Soft Drinks 1

Business Equipment 1

Packaged goods/cosmetics 2

Healthcare Sector (3 subsectors, 6 firms)

Medical instruments 1

Pharmaceutical 3

Medical/Industrial diversified 2

Technology Sector (7 subsectors, 12 firms)

Computer software: Prepackaged 2

Computer software: Programming/Internet 2

Technical & System Software 1

Communications Equipment 2

Semiconductor:

     Integrated Circuits 1

     Broad Line 1

Telecommunications equipment 3

***

REPORTS

BASIC MATERIALS SECTOR

Oil & gas production

Subsector	Oil & gas production
Most Recent FY	**2013 Dec 31**
Observation Period:	6 years

Note: *Dispersion refers to the sample standard deviation, assuming normality. However the probability distribution may differ and the normal approximation may not be valid.*

1. CASH DIVIDEND GROWTH

Average growth over period	2.0%
Dispersion	12%

*Dividends are actual amounts reported.

Year-over-year dividend growth rates :

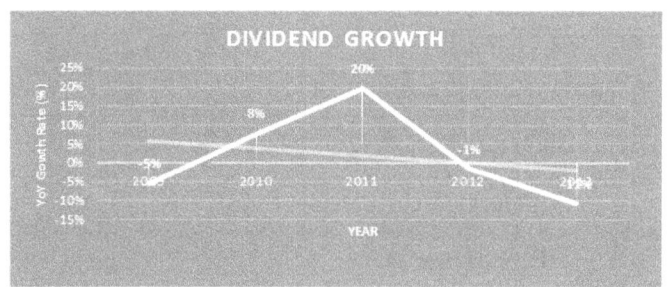

2. DIVIDEND COVERAGE RATIO

Average over period	-0.14
Dispersion	0.75

Dividend coverage for each year:

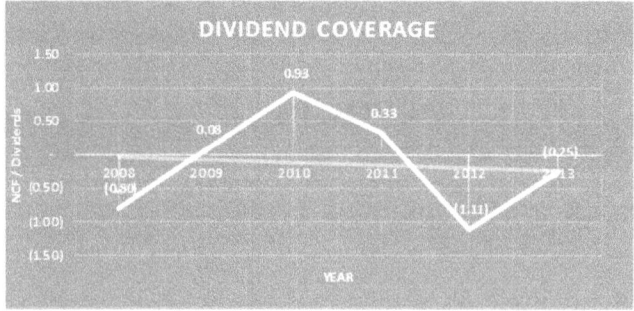

116

3. NET CASH FLOW (NCF) RATIO

Average over period	-0.01
Dispersion	0.03

Net cash flow relative to revenues for each year:

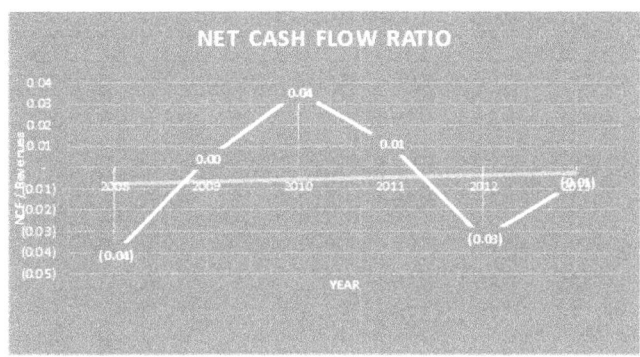

4. Components of NCF

Net cash from operations (NCO), Capital expenditures (Capex).	NCO	CAPEX
Average for period	0.17	0.17
Dispersion	0.06	0.05

Main components of NCF relative to revenues, for each year:

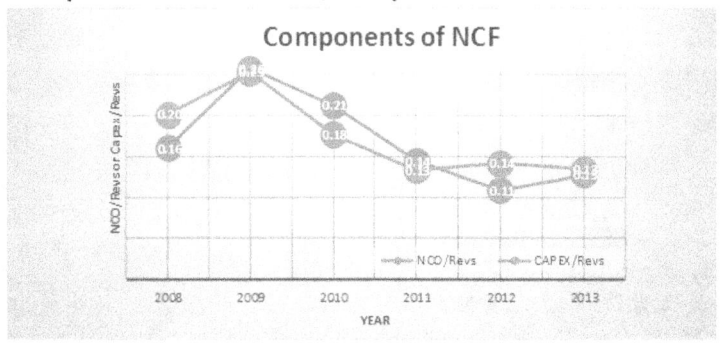

116

23

Subsector	Oil & gas production
Most Recent FY	2014 to June 30
Observation Period:	6 years

Note: *Dispersion refers to the sample standard deviation, assuming normality. However the probability distribution may differ and the normal approximation may not be valid.*

1. CASH DIVIDEND GROWTH

Average growth over period	15.6%
Dispersion	26%

*Dividends are actual amounts reported.

Year-over-year dividend growth rates :

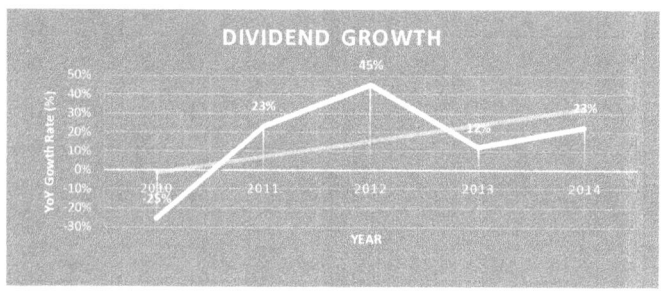

2. DIVIDEND COVERAGE RATIO

Average over period	1.05
Dispersion	0.77

Dividend coverage for each year:

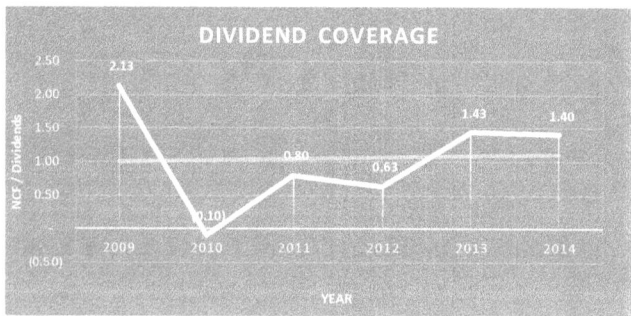

118

3. NET CASH FLOW (NCF) RATIO

Average over period	0.06
Dispersion	0.04

Net cash flow relative to revenues for each year:

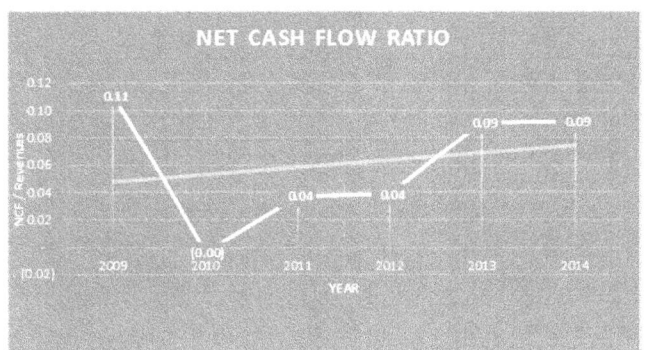

4. Components of NCF

Net cash from operations (NCO), Capital expenditures (Capex).	NCO	CAPEX
Average for period	0.22	0.16
Dispersion	0.06	0.03

Main components of NCF relative to revenues, for each year:

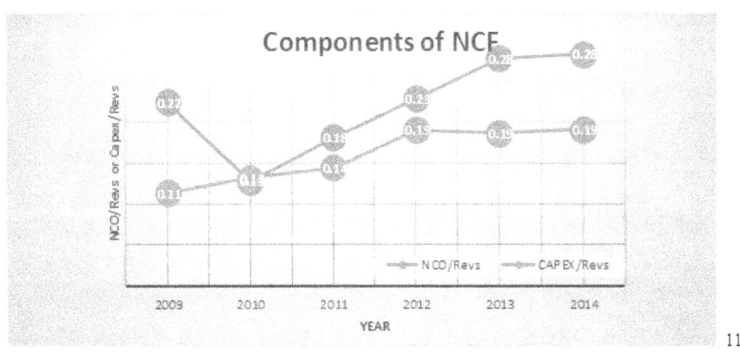

118

Note: *Financial statements were restated for FY 2012 and 2013.*

***

25

Independent Oil & Gas Production

Subsector   **Independent Oil & Gas Production**

Most Recent FY   **2013 to Dec 31**

Observation Period: 6 years

Note: *Dispersion refers to the sample standard deviation, assuming normality. However the probability distribution may differ and the normal approximation may not be valid.*

1. CASH DIVIDEND GROWTH

Average growth over period	20.6%
Dispersion	10%

*Dividends are actual amounts reported.

Year-over-year dividend growth rates :

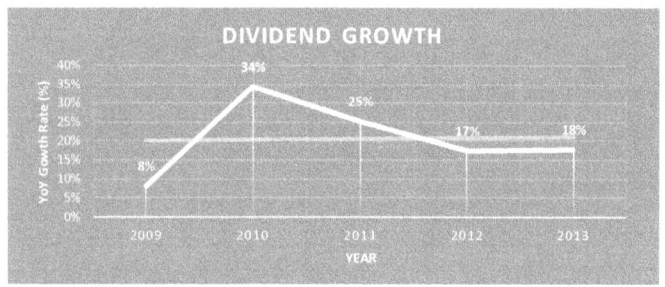

2. DIVIDEND COVERAGE RATIO

Average over period	2.40
Dispersion	5.39

Dividend coverage for each year:

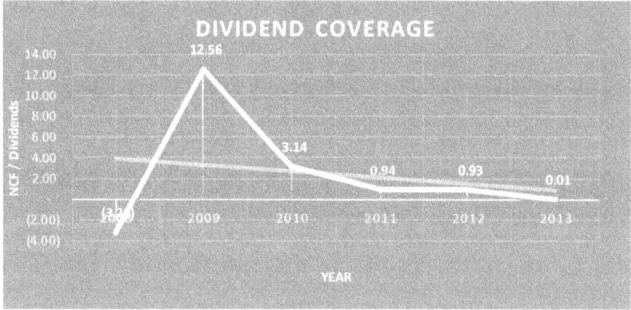

3. NET CASH FLOW (NCF) RATIO

Average over period	0.06
Dispersion	0.11

Net cash flow relative to revenues for each year:

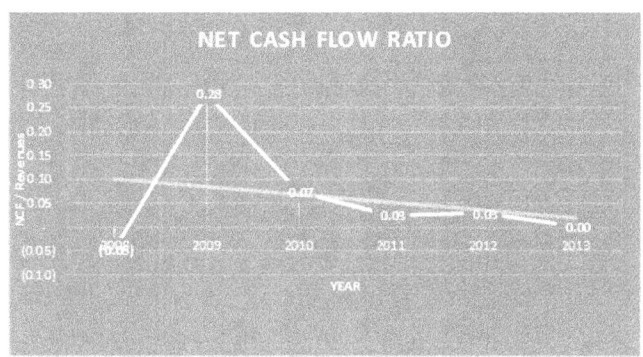

4. Components of NCF

Net cash from operations (NCO), Capital expenditures (Capex).	NCO	CAPEX
Average for period	0.48	0.42
Dispersion	0.05	0.07

Main components of NCF relative to revenues, for each year:

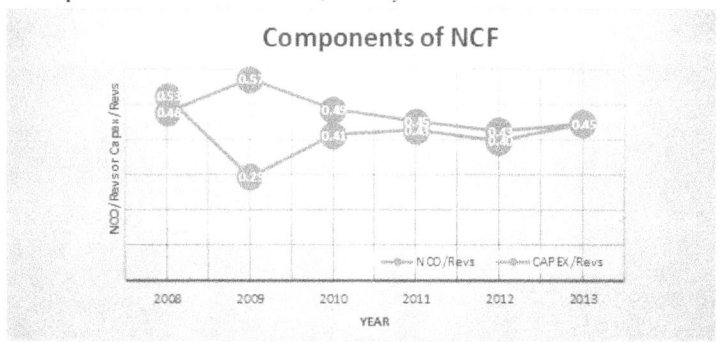

117

***

27

Integrated oil companies

Subsector	**Oil-Integrated oil companies**
Most Recent FY	**2013 to Dec 31**
Observation Period:	6 years

Note: *Dispersion refers to the sample standard deviation, assuming normality. However the probability distribution may differ and the normal approximation may not be valid.*

1. CASH DIVIDEND GROWTH

Average growth over period	#DIV/0!
Dispersion	#DIV/0!

*Dividends are actual amounts reported.

Year-over-year dividend growth rates :   Dividend payments began in FY 2011

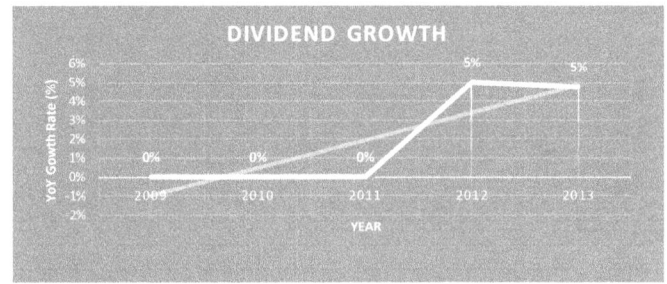

2. DIVIDEND COVERAGE RATIO

Average over period	#DIV/0!
Dispersion	#DIV/0!

Dividend coverage for each year:

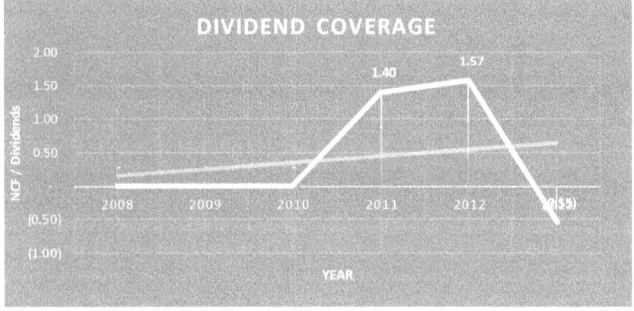

119

3. NET CASH FLOW (NCF) RATIO

Average over period	0.02
Dispersion	0.03

Net cash flow relative to revenues for each year:

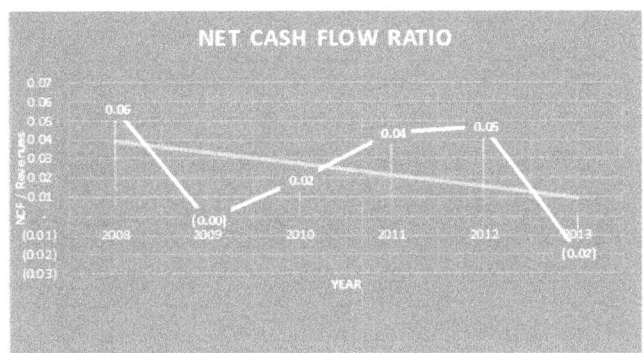

4. Components of NCF

Net cash from operations (NCO), Capital expenditures (Capex).	NCO	CAPEX
Average for period	0.17	0.14
Dispersion	0.01	0.03

Main components of NCF relative to revenues, for each year:

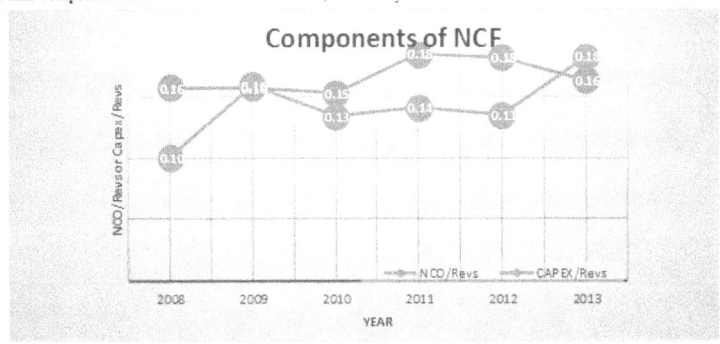

119

29

Subsector	Oil-Integrated oil companies
Most Recent FY	**2013 to Dec 31**
Observation Period:	6 years

Note: *Dispersion refers to the sample standard deviation, assuming normality. However the probability distribution may differ and the normal approximation may not be valid.*

1. CASH DIVIDEND GROWTH

Average growth over period	7.7%
Dispersion	3%

*Dividends are actual amounts reported.

Year-over-year dividend growth rates :

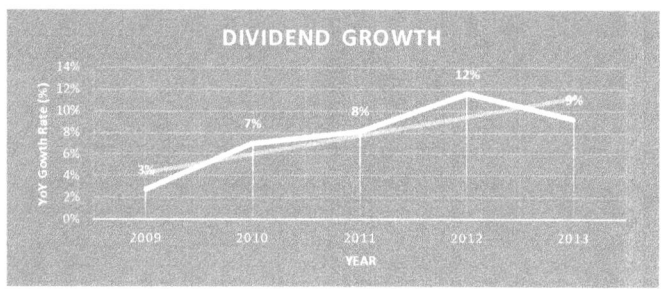

2. DIVIDEND COVERAGE RATIO

Average over period	1.17
Dispersion	1.17

Dividend coverage for each year:

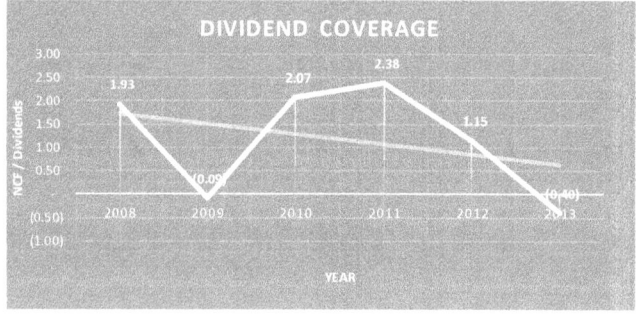

3. NET CASH FLOW (NCF) RATIO

Average over period	0.03
Dispersion	0.03

Net cash flow relative to revenues for each year:

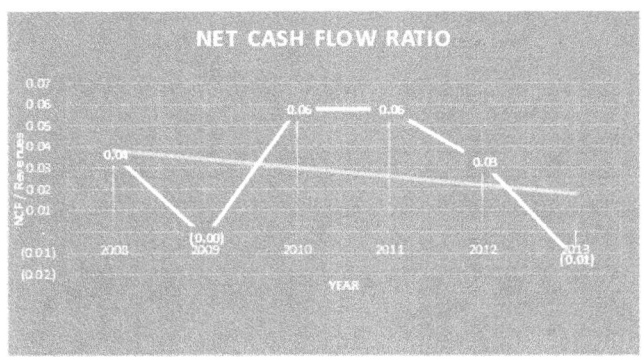

4. Components of NCF

Net cash from operations (NCO), Capital expenditures (Capex).	NCO	CAPEX
Average for period	0.14	0.11
Dispersion	0.02	0.03

Main components of NCF relative to revenues, for each year:

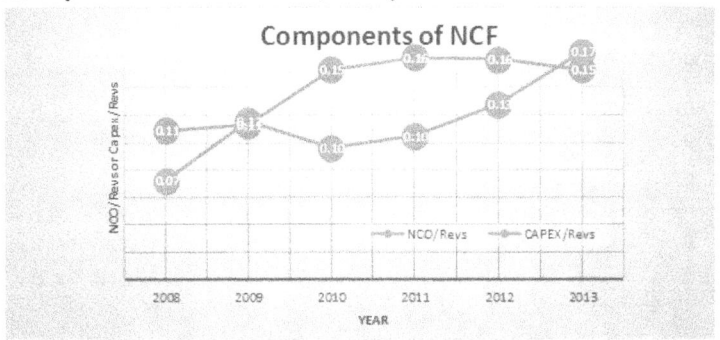

120

***

CONSUMER GOODS SECTOR

Auto manufacturing

Subsector   **Auto manufacturing**
Most Recent FY   **2014 to Mar 31**
Observation Period: 6 years

Note: *Dispersion refers to the sample standard deviation, assuming normality. However the probability distribution may differ and the normal approximation may not be valid.*

1. CASH DIVIDEND GROWTH

Average growth over period	3.8%
Dispersion	32%

*Dividends are actual amounts reported.

Year-over-year dividend growth rates :

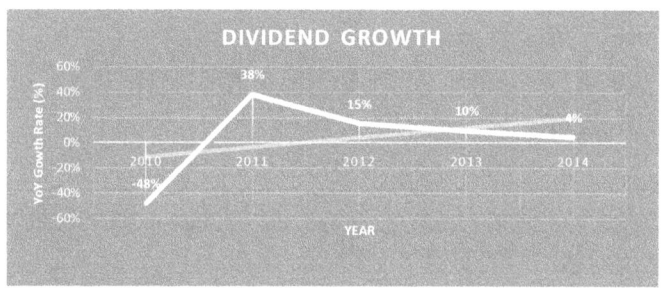

2. DIVIDEND COVERAGE RATIO

Average over period	4.58
Dispersion	5.73

Dividend coverage for each year:

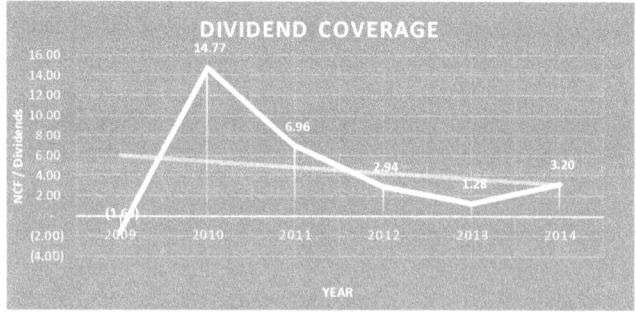

3. NET CASH FLOW (NCF) RATIO

Average over period	0.05
Dispersion	0.05

Net cash flow relative to revenues for each year:

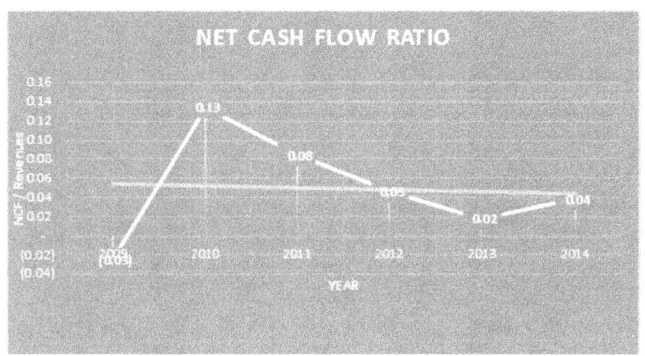

4. Components of NCF

Net cash from operations (NCO), Capital expenditures (Capex).	NCO	CAPEX
Average for period	0.10	0.05
Dispersion	0.05	0.01

Main components of NCF relative to revenues, for each year:

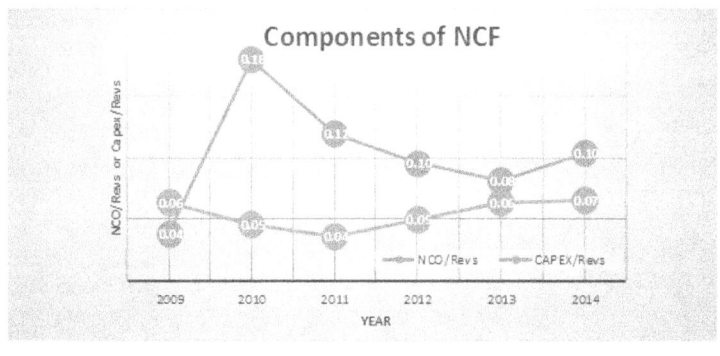

101

Subsector	Auto manufacturing
Most Recent FY	2014 to Mar 31
Observation Period:	6 years

Note: *Dispersion refers to the sample standard deviation, assuming normality. However the probability distribution may differ and the normal approximation may not be valid.*

1. CASH DIVIDEND GROWTH

Average growth over period	34.6%
Dispersion	119%

*Dividends are actual amounts reported.

Year-over-year dividend growth rates :

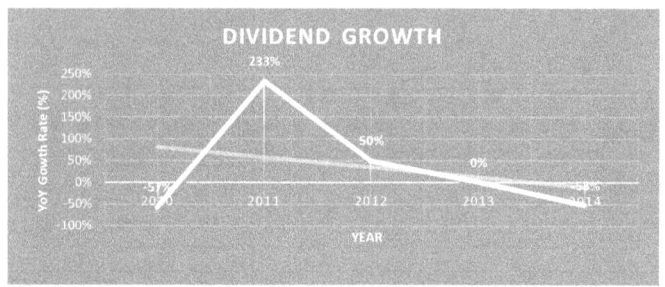

2. DIVIDEND COVERAGE RATIO

Average over period	15.10
Dispersion	14.08

Dividend coverage for each year:

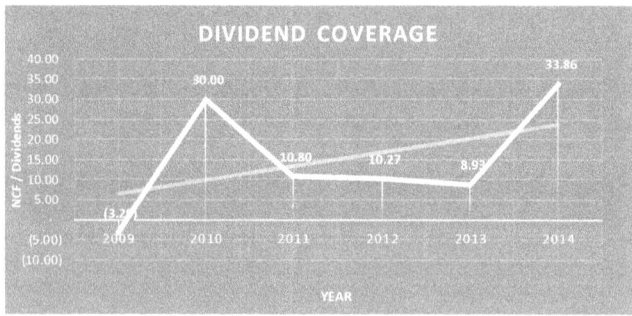

3. NET CASH FLOW (NCF) RATIO

Average over period	0.07
Dispersion	0.05

Net cash flow relative to revenues for each year:

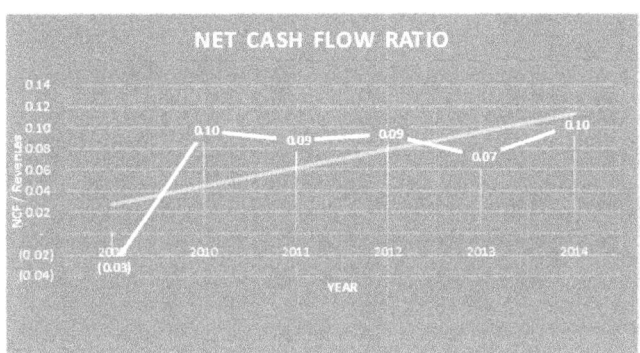

4. Components of NCF

Net cash from operations (NCO), Capital expenditures (Capex).	NCO	CAPEX
Average for period	0.12	0.05
Dispersion	0.04	0.01

Main components of NCF relative to revenues, for each year:

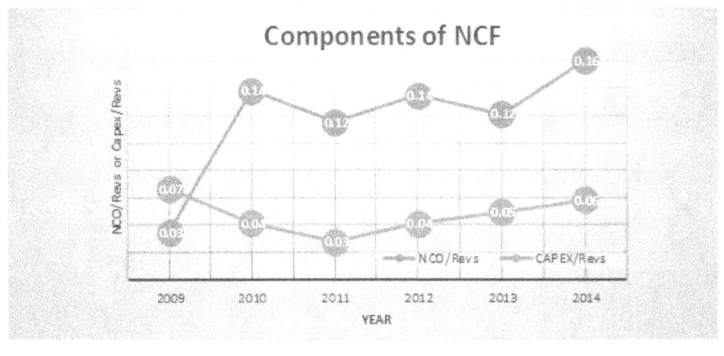

103

35

Subsector	Auto manufacturing
Most Recent FY	2013 to Dec 31
Observation Period:	6 years

Note: *Dispersion refers to the sample standard deviation, assuming normality. However the probability distribution may differ and the normal approximation may not be valid.*

1. CASH DIVIDEND GROWTH

Average growth over period	#DIV/0!
Dispersion	#DIV/0!

*Dividends are actual amounts reported.

Year-over-year dividend growth rates : Dividend payments reported from FY 2012

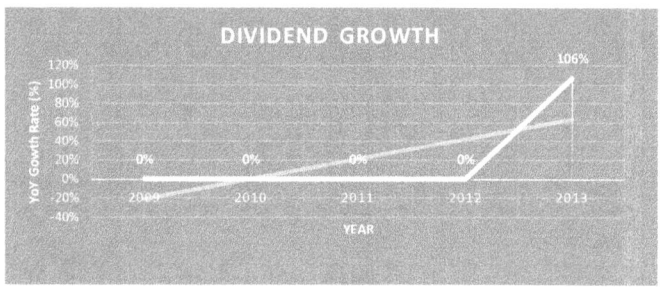

2. DIVIDEND COVERAGE RATIO

Average over period	#DIV/0!
Dispersion	#DIV/0!

Dividend coverage for each year:

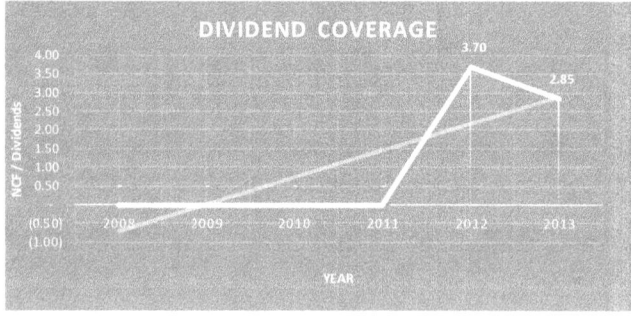

102

3. NET CASH FLOW (NCF) RATIO

Average over period	0.02
Dispersion	0.04

Net cash flow relative to revenues for each year:

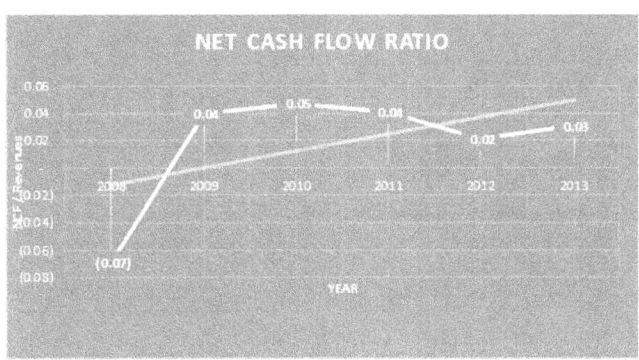

4. Components of NCF

Net cash from operations (NCO), Capital expenditures (Capex).	NCO	CAPEX
Average for period	0.06	0.04
Dispersion	0.02	0.01

Main components of NCF relative to revenues, for each year:

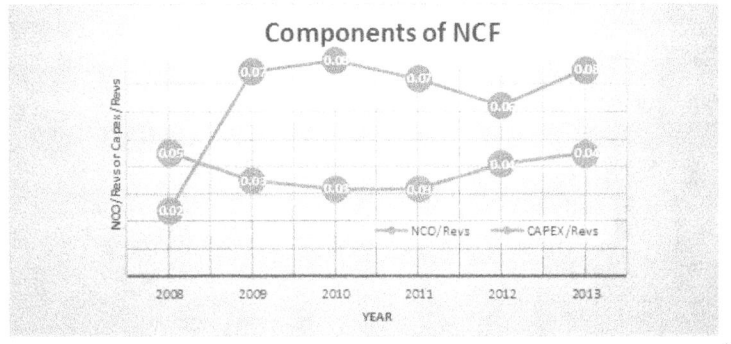

102

Note: *Data discrepancies in financial statements for Net Cash from Operations during observation period.*

***

37

Beverages-Production & Distribution

Subsector	Beverages-Wineries & Distillers
Most Recent FY	2014 to June 30
Observation Period:	6 years

Note: *Dispersion refers to the sample standard deviation, assuming normality. However the probability distribution may differ and the normal approximation may not be valid.*

1. CASH DIVIDEND GROWTH

Average growth over period	7.1%
Dispersion	2%

*Dividends are actual amounts reported.

Year-over-year dividend growth rates :

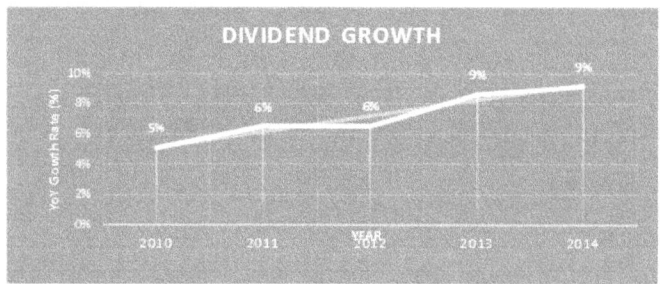

2. DIVIDEND COVERAGE RATIO

Average over period	1.50
Dispersion	0.40

Dividend coverage for each year:

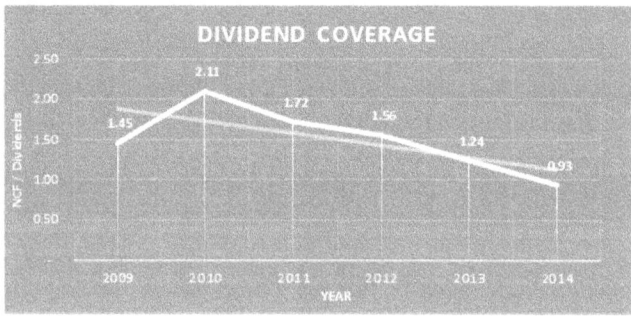

104

38

3. NET CASH FLOW (NCF) RATIO

Average over period	0.15
Dispersion	0.03

Net cash flow relative to revenues for each year:

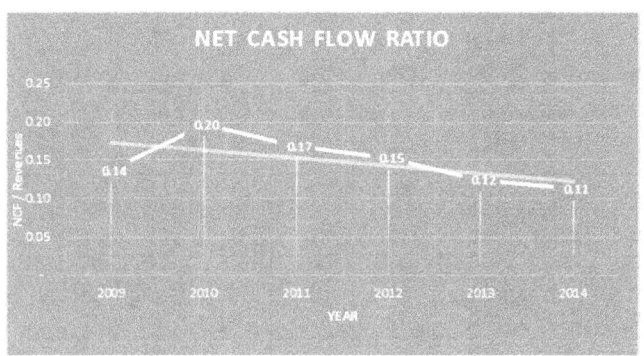

4. Components of NCF

Net cash from operations (NCO), Capital expenditures (Capex).	NCO	CAPEX
Average for period	0.20	0.05
Dispersion	0.02	0.01

Main components of NCF relative to revenues, for each year:

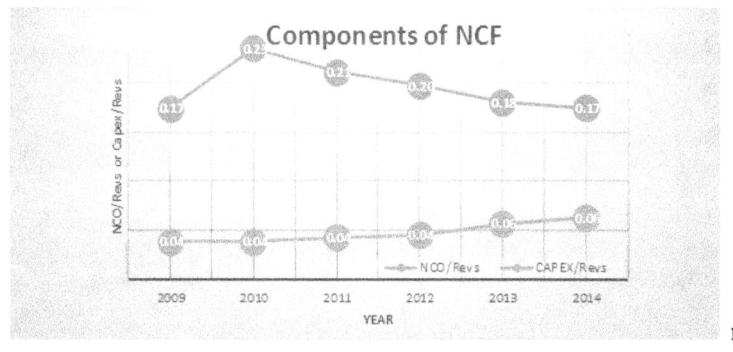

104

Note: *Financial statements were restated for 2013 and 2012.*

Subsector	Beverages-Brewers
Most Recent FY	2013 to Dec 31
Observation Period:	6 years

Note: *Dispersion refers to the sample standard deviation, assuming normality. However the probability distribution may differ and the normal approximation may not be valid.*

1. CASH DIVIDEND GROWTH

Average growth over period	54.2%
Dispersion	30%

Dividends are actual amounts reported.

Year-over-year dividend growth rates :

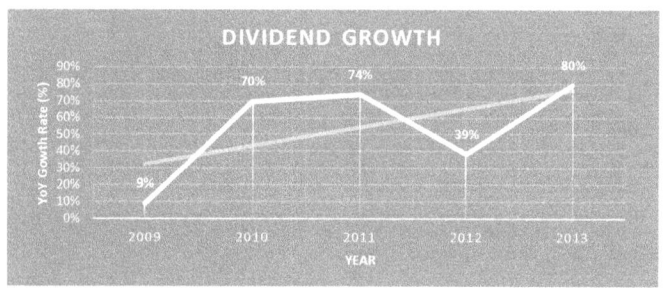

2. DIVIDEND COVERAGE RATIO

Average over period	4.19
Dispersion	4.10

Dividend coverage for each year:

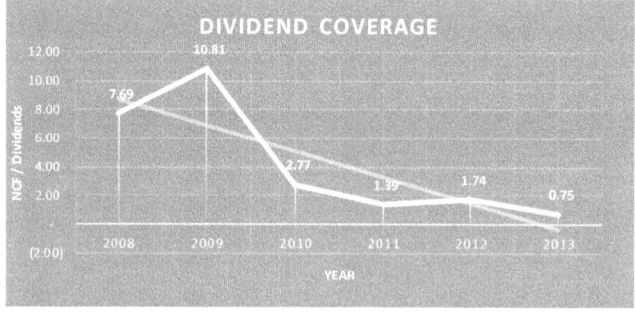

3. NET CASH FLOW (NCF) RATIO

Average over period	0.08
Dispersion	0.04

Net cash flow relative to revenues for each year:

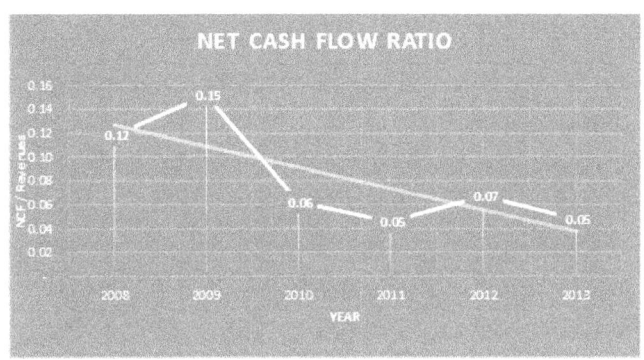

4. Components of NCF

Net cash from operations (NCO), Capital expenditures (Capex).	NCO	CAPEX
Average for period	0.14	0.06
Dispersion	0.04	0.01

Main components of NCF relative to revenues, for each year:

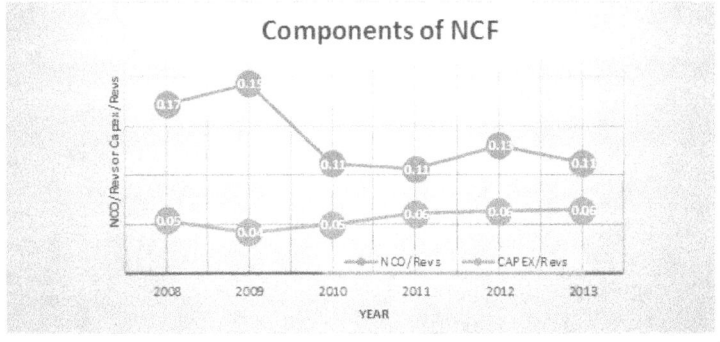

41

Subsector	**Beverages-Soft Drinks**
Most Recent FY	**2013 to Dec 31**
Observation Period:	6 years

Note: *Dispersion refers to the sample standard deviation, assuming normality. However the probability distribution may differ and the normal approximation may not be valid.*

1. CASH DIVIDEND GROWTH

Average growth over period	7.1%
Dispersion	1%

*Dividends are actual amounts reported.

Year-over-year dividend growth rates :

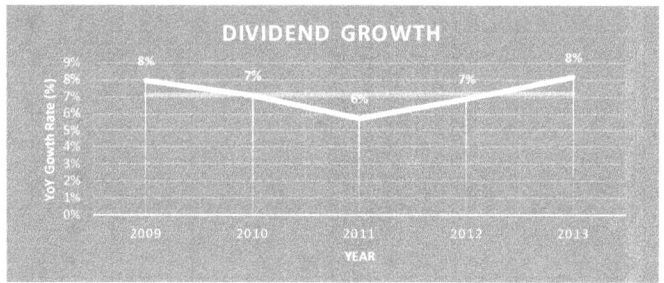

2. DIVIDEND COVERAGE RATIO

Average over period	1.64
Dispersion	0.10

Dividend coverage for each year:

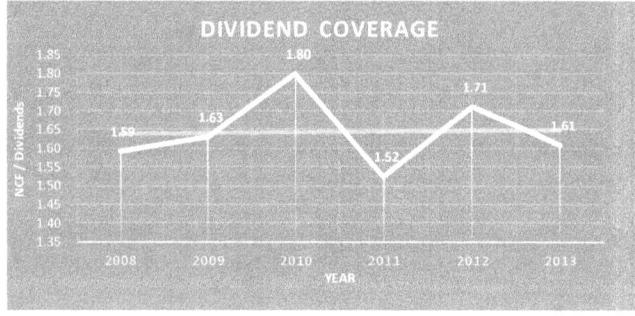

106

3. NET CASH FLOW (NCF) RATIO

Average over period	0.18
Dispersion	0.02

Net cash flow relative to revenues for each year:

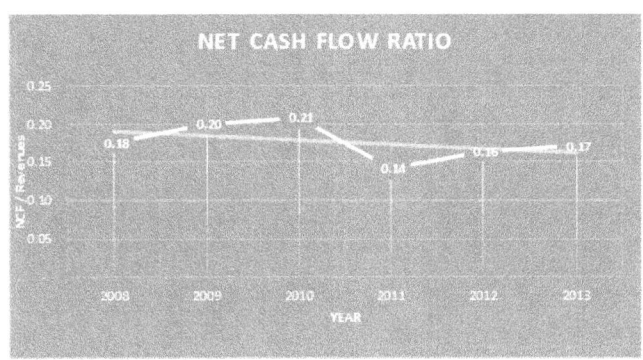

4. Components of NCF

Net cash from operations (NCO), Capital expenditures (Capex).	NCO	CAPEX
Average for period	0.24	0.06
Dispersion	0.03	0.00

Main components of NCF relative to revenues, for each year:

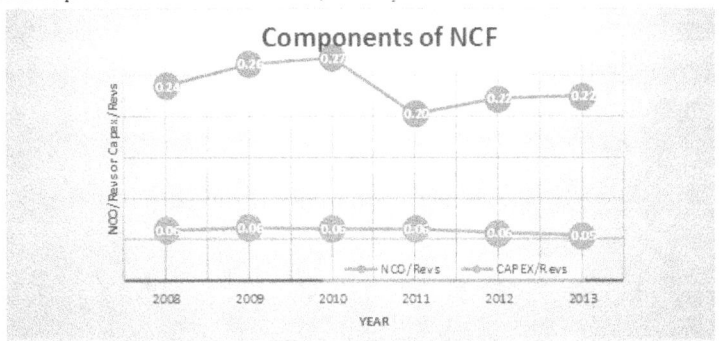

106

***

Business Equipment

Subsector   **Industrial machinery and components**
Most Recent FY   **2013 to Dec 31**
Observation Period: 6 years

Note: *Dispersion refers to the sample standard deviation, assuming normality. However the probability distribution may differ and the normal approximation may not be valid.*

1. CASH DIVIDEND GROWTH

Average growth over period	1.8%
Dispersion	9%

Dividends are actual amounts reported.

Year-over-year dividend growth rates :

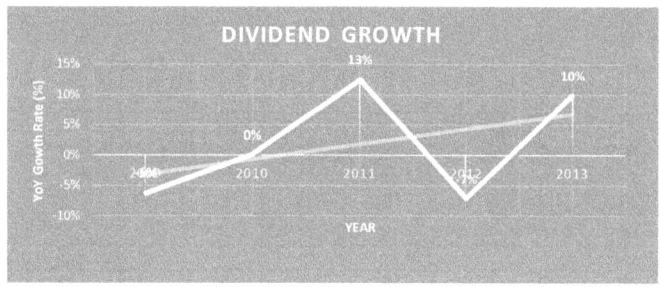

2. DIVIDEND COVERAGE RATIO

Average over period	1.86
Dispersion	1.18

Dividend coverage for each year:

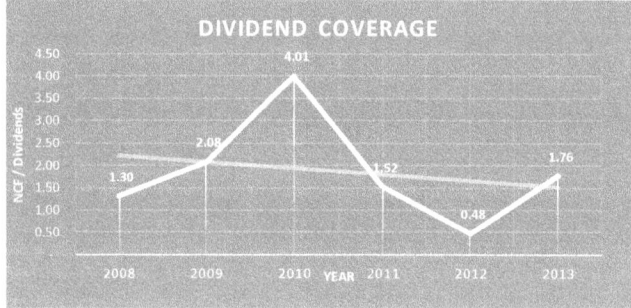

3. NET CASH FLOW (NCF) RATIO

Average over period	0.07
Dispersion	0.04

Net cash flow relative to revenues for each year:

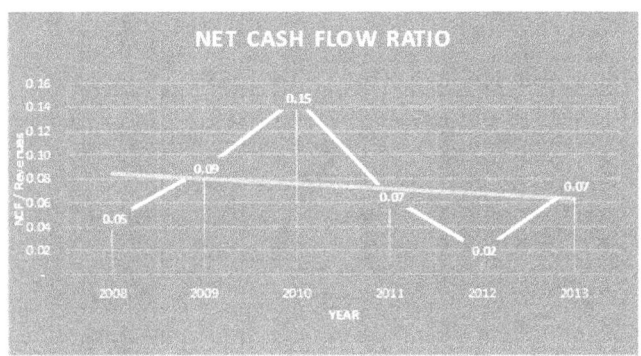

4. Components of NCF

Net cash from operations (NCO), Capital expenditures (Capex)	NCO	CAPEX
Average for period	0.15	0.08
Dispersion	0.04	0.02

Main components of NCF relative to revenues, for each year:

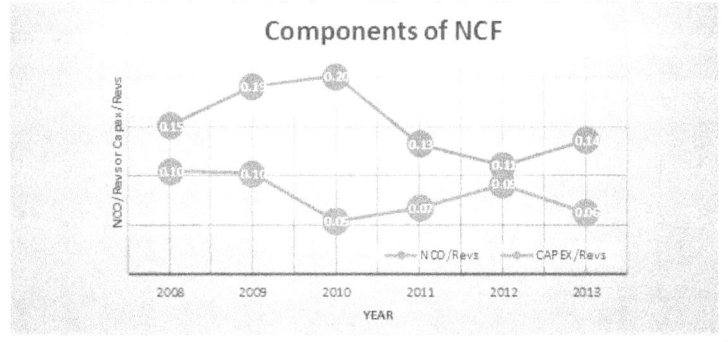

112

***

45

Packaged goods/cosmetics

Subsector	Packaged goods/cosmetics
Most Recent FY	2013 to Dec 31
Observation Period:	6 years

Note: *Dispersion refers to the sample standard deviation, assuming normality. However the probability distribution may differ and the normal approximation may not be valid.*

1. CASH DIVIDEND GROWTH

Average growth over period	7.5%
Dispersion	4%

*Dividends are actual amounts reported.

Year-over-year dividend growth rates :

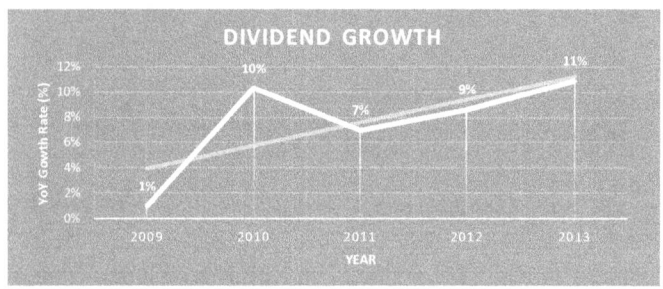

2. DIVIDEND COVERAGE RATIO

Average over period	1.61
Dispersion	0.30

Dividend coverage for each year:

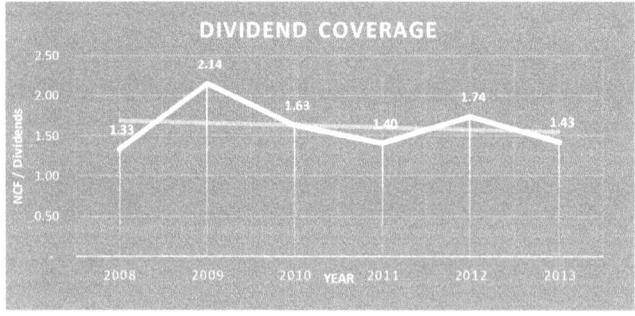

121

3. NET CASH FLOW (NCF) RATIO

Average over period	0.09
Dispersion	0.02

Net cash flow relative to revenues for each year:

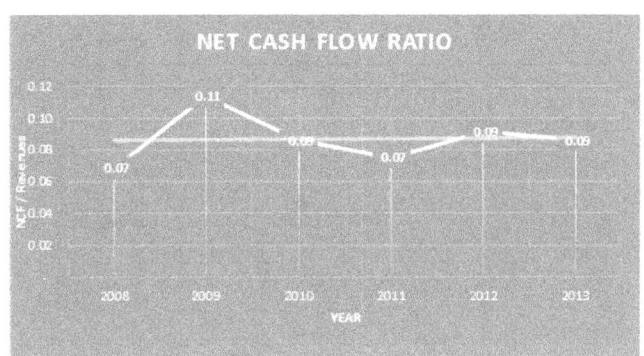

4. Components of NCF

Net cash from operations (NCO), Capital expenditures (Capex).	NCO	CAPEX
Average for period	0.12	0.04
Dispersion	0.02	0.01

Main components of NCF relative to revenues, for each year:

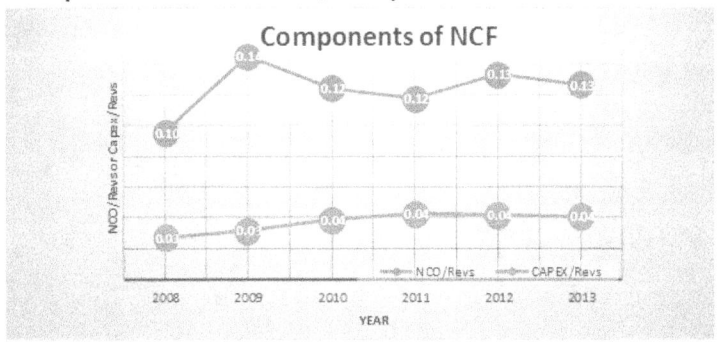

121

47

Subsector	Packaged goods/cosmetics
Most Recent FY	2014 to June 30
Observation Period:	6 years

Note: *Dispersion refers to the sample standard deviation, assuming normality. However the probability distribution may differ and the normal approximation may not be valid.*

1. CASH DIVIDEND GROWTH

Average growth over period	6.5%
Dispersion	1%

*Dividends are actual amounts reported.

Year-over-year dividend growth rates :

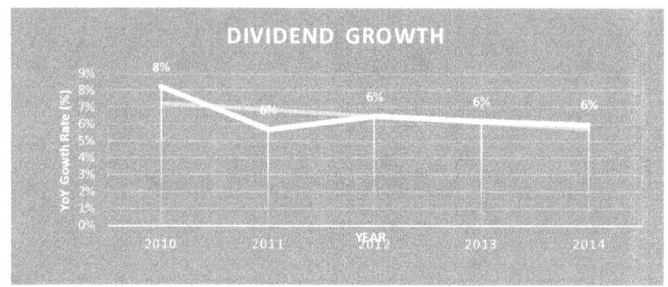

2. DIVIDEND COVERAGE RATIO

Average over period	1.84
Dispersion	0.40

Dividend coverage for each year:

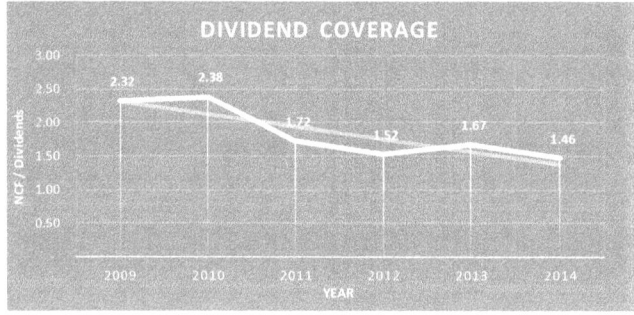

122

3. NET CASH FLOW (NCF) RATIO

Average over period	0.13
Dispersion	0.02

Net cash flow relative to revenues for each year:

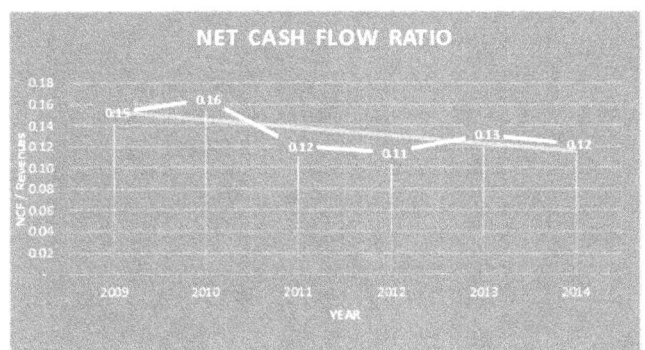

4. Components of NCF

Net cash from operations (NCO), Capital expenditures (Capex).	NCO	CAPEX
Average for period	0.18	0.04
Dispersion	0.02	0.00

Main components of NCF relative to revenues, for each year:

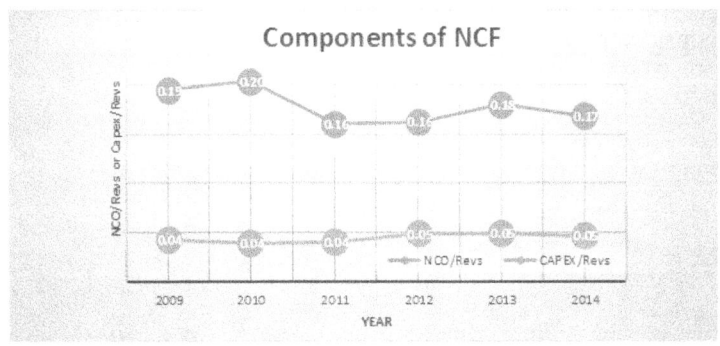

122

***

49

HEALTHCARE SECTOR

Medical instruments

Subsector   **Medical/dental instruments**
Most Recent FY   **2014 to Sept 26**
Observation Period: 6 years

Note: Dispersion refers to the sample standard deviation, assuming normality. However the probability distribution may differ and the normal approximation may not be valid.

1. CASH DIVIDEND GROWTH

Average growth over period	12.5%
Dispersion	4%

*Dividends are actual amounts reported.

Year-over-year dividend growth rates :

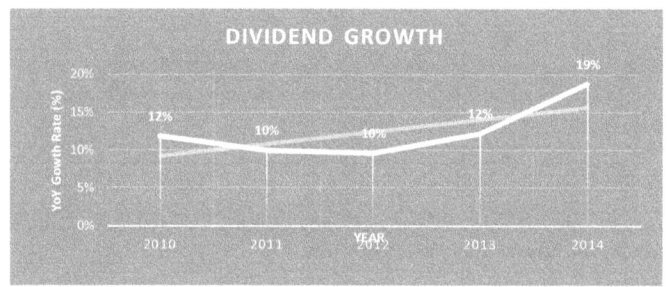

2. DIVIDEND COVERAGE RATIO

Average over period	4.06
Dispersion	0.79

Dividend coverage for each year:

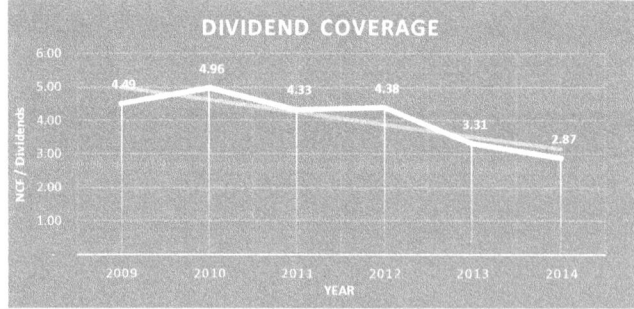

114

50

3. NET CASH FLOW (NCF) RATIO

Average over period	0.16
Dispersion	0.02

Net cash flow relative to revenues for each year:

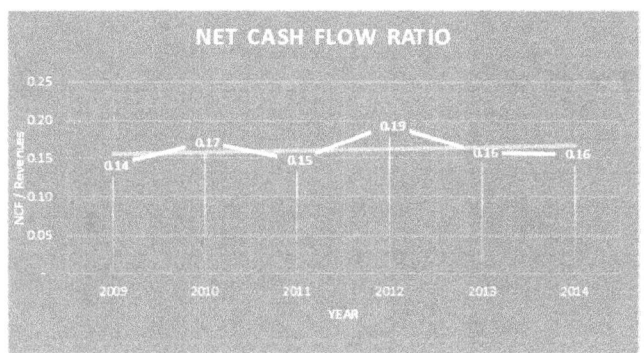

4. Components of NCF

Net cash from operations (NCO), Capital expenditures (Capex).	NCO	CAPEX
Average for period	0.20	0.04
Dispersion	0.02	0.01

Main components of NCF relative to revenues, for each year:

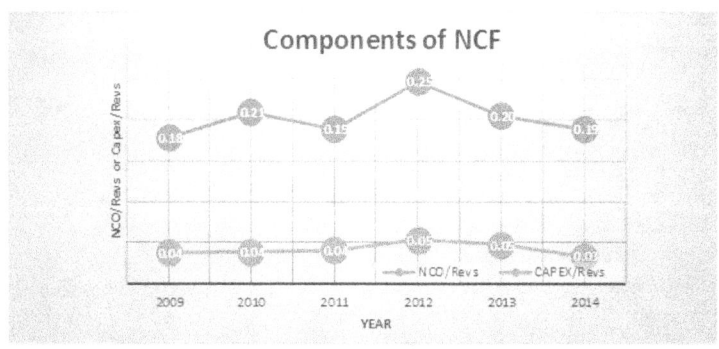

114

Note: *Revised 2012 revenues figure used as reported in FY 2014 financial statements.*

***

Pharmaceutical

Subsector	Pharmaceutical
Most Recent FY	2013 to Dec 31
Observation Period:	6 years

Note: *Dispersion refers to the sample standard deviation, assuming normality. However the probability distribution may differ and the normal approximation may not be valid.*

1. CASH DIVIDEND GROWTH

Average growth over period	23.4%
Dispersion	11%

Dividends are actual amounts reported.

Year-over-year dividend growth rates :

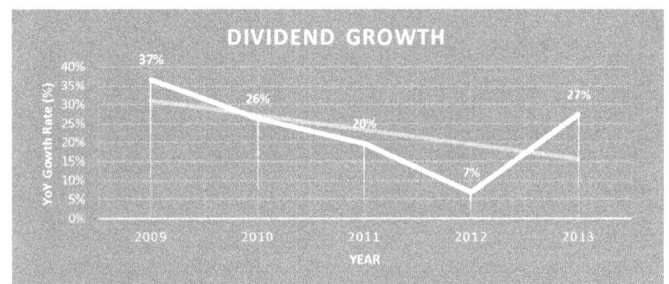

2. DIVIDEND COVERAGE RATIO

Average over period	4.44
Dispersion	1.53

Dividend coverage for each year:

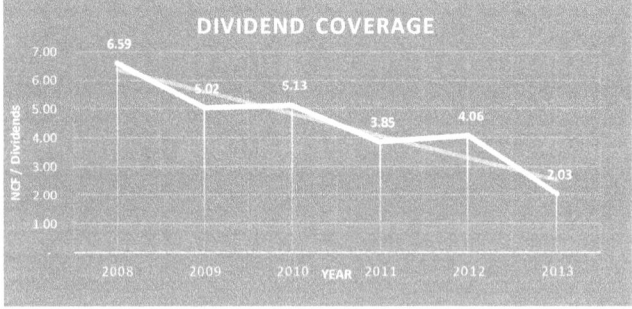

3. NET CASH FLOW (NCF) RATIO

Average over period	0.18
Dispersion	0.04

Net cash flow relative to revenues for each year:

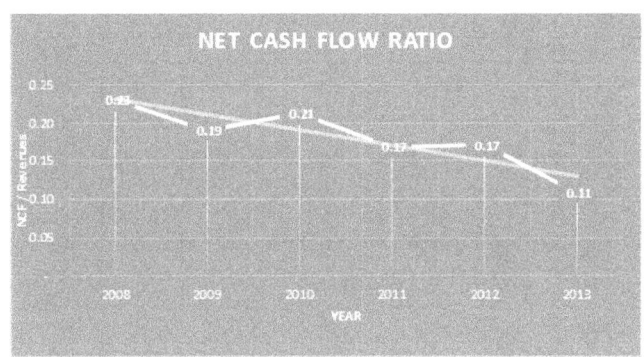

4. Components of NCF

Net cash from operations (NCO), Capital expenditures (Capex).

	NCO	CAPEX
Average for period	0.23	0.05
Dispersion	0.04	0.01

Main components of NCF relative to revenues, for each year:

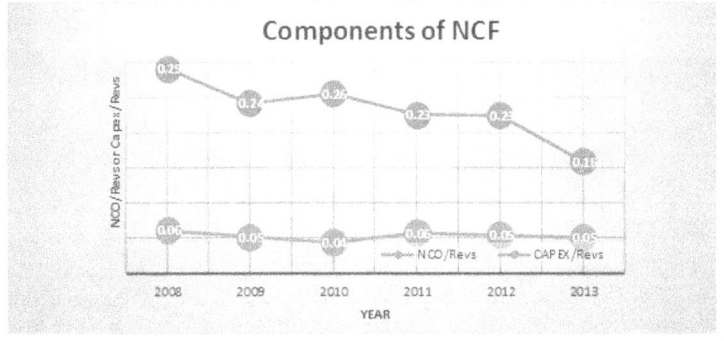

123

Subsector	Pharmaceutical
Most Recent FY	2013 to Dec 31
Observation Period:	6 years

Note: *Dispersion refers to the sample standard deviation, assuming normality. However the probability distribution may differ and the normal approximation may not be valid.*

1. CASH DIVIDEND GROWTH

Average growth over period	23.5%
Dispersion	78%

*Dividends are actual amounts reported.

Year-over-year dividend growth rates :

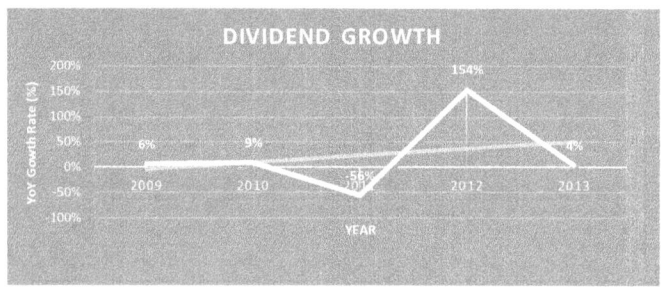

2. DIVIDEND COVERAGE RATIO

Average over period	2.74
Dispersion	1.41

Dividend coverage for each year:

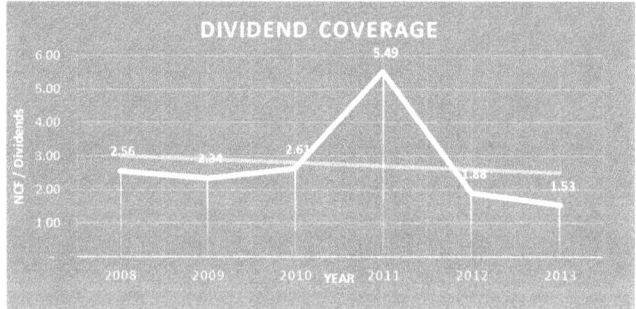

124

3. NET CASH FLOW (NCF) RATIO

Average over period	0.22
Dispersion	0.04

Net cash flow relative to revenues for each year:

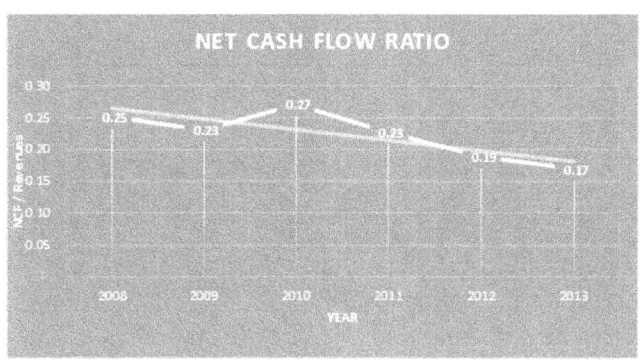

4. Components of NCF

Net cash from operations (NCO), Capital expenditures (Capex).	NCO	CAPEX
Average for period	0.27	0.05
Dispersion	0.04	0.01

Main components of NCF relative to revenues, for each year:

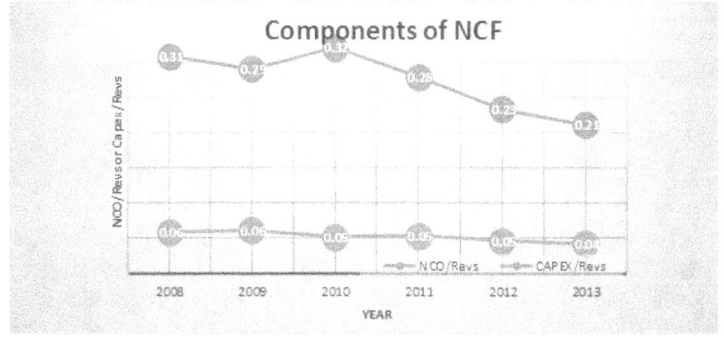

124

55

Subsector	Pharmaceutical
Most Recent FY	2013 to Dec 31
Observation Period:	6 years

Note: *Dispersion refers to the sample standard deviation, assuming normality. However the probability distribution may differ and the normal approximation may not be valid.*

1. CASH DIVIDEND GROWTH

Average growth over period	-3.5%
Dispersion	18%

Dividends are actual amounts reported.

Year-over-year dividend growth rates :

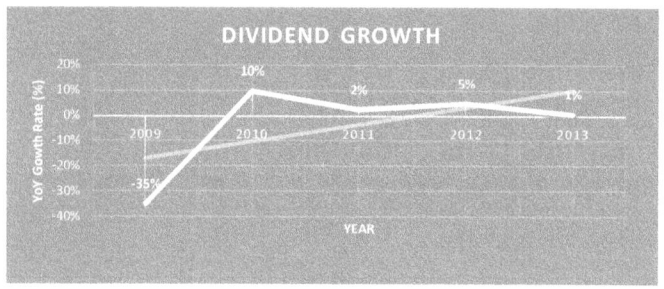

2. DIVIDEND COVERAGE RATIO

Average over period	2.37
Dispersion	0.51

Dividend coverage for each year:

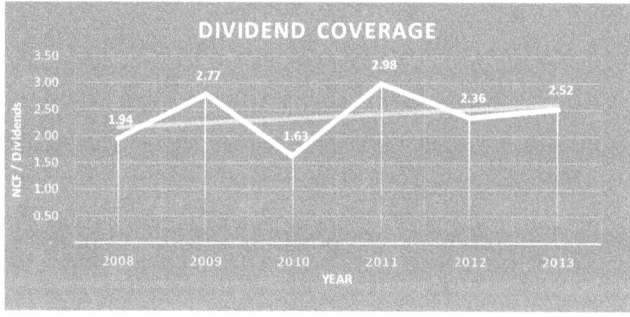

125

56

3. NET CASH FLOW (NCF) RATIO

Average over period	0.28
Dispersion	0.07

Net cash flow relative to revenues for each year:

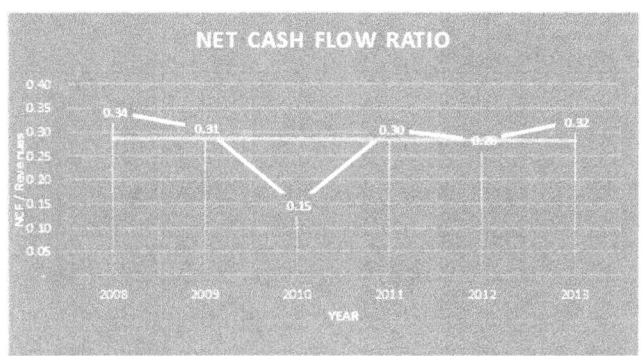

4. Components of NCF

Net cash from operations (NCO), Capital expenditures (Capex).	NCO	CAPEX
Average for period	0.31	0.03
Dispersion	0.07	0.00

Main components of NCF relative to revenues, for each year:

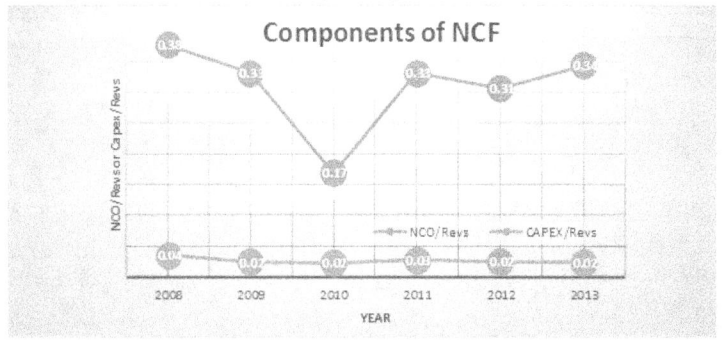

***

Medical/Industrial diversified

Subsector	Medical/Industrial Diversifed
Most Recent FY	2013 to Dec 31
Observation Period:	6 years

Note: *Dispersion refers to the sample standard deviation, assuming normality. However the probability distribution may differ and the normal approximation may not be valid.*

1. CASH DIVIDEND GROWTH

Average growth over period	4.4%
Dispersion	1%

*Dividends are actual amounts reported.

Year-over-year dividend growth rates :

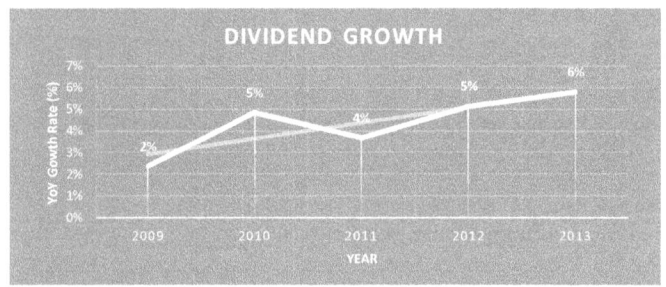

2. DIVIDEND COVERAGE RATIO

Average over period	2.50
Dispersion	0.24

Dividend coverage for each year:

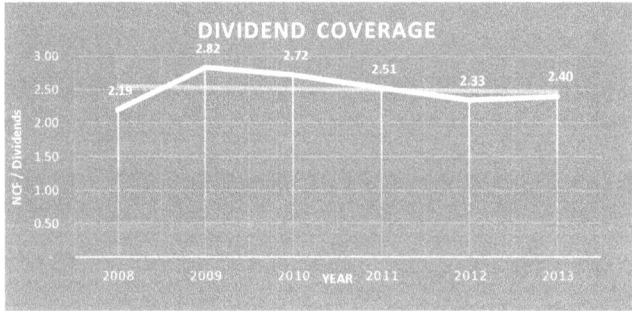

3. NET CASH FLOW (NCF) RATIO

Average over period	0.14
Dispersion	0.02

Net cash flow relative to revenues for each year:

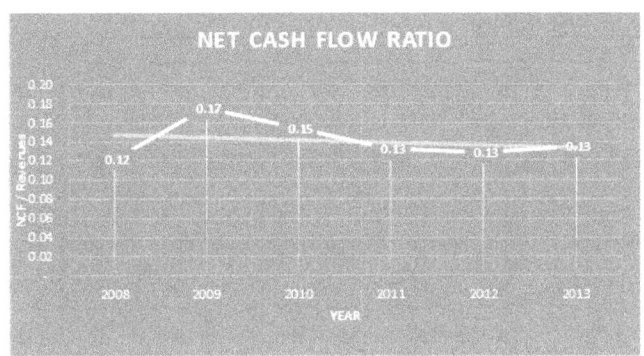

4. Components of NCF

Net cash from operations (NCO), Capital expenditures (Capex).	NCO	CAPEX
Average for period	0.19	0.05
Dispersion	0.01	0.01

Main components of NCF relative to revenues, for each year:

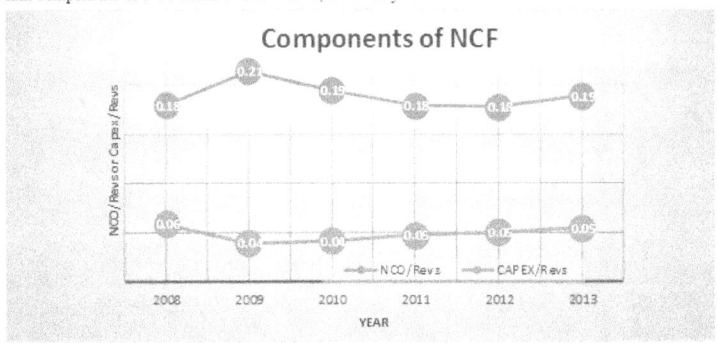

115

Note: *Business includes diversified machinery.*

Subsector	Medical/Industrial Diversified
Most Recent FY	**2013 to Dec 31**
Observation Period:	6 years

Note: *Dispersion refers to the sample standard deviation, assuming normality. However the probability distribution may differ and the normal approximation may not be valid.*

1. CASH DIVIDEND GROWTH

Average growth over period	#DIV/0!
Dispersion	#DIV/0!

Dividends are actual amounts reported.

Year-over-year dividend growth rates : Dividend payments began in FY 2012

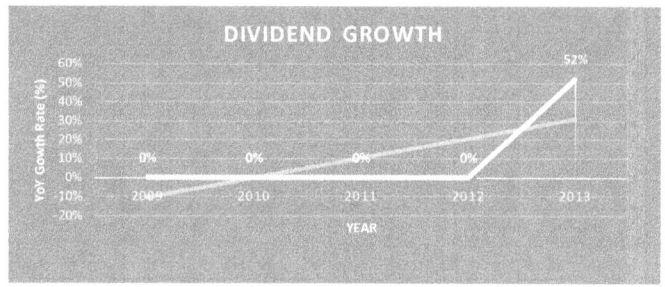

2. DIVIDEND COVERAGE RATIO

Average over period	#DIV/0!
Dispersion	#DIV/0!

Dividend coverage for each year:

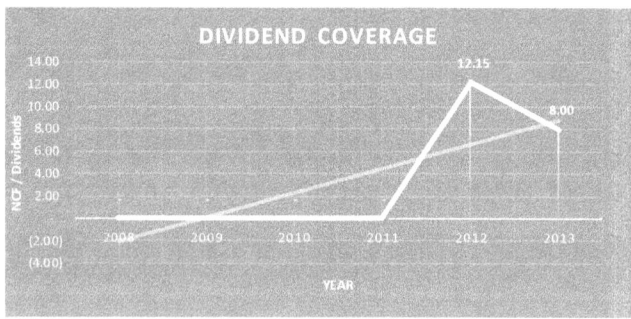

113

60

3. NET CASH FLOW (NCF) RATIO

Average over period	0.13
Dispersion	0.01

Net cash flow relative to revenues for each year:

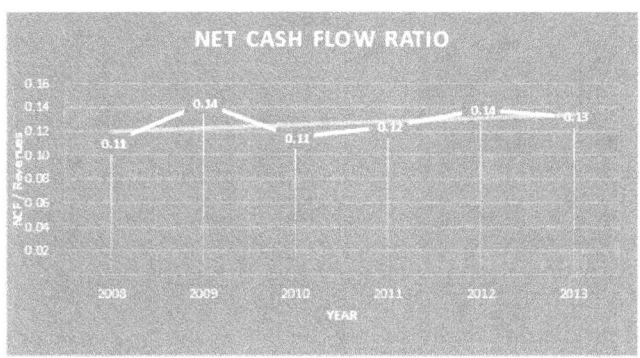

4. Components of NCF

Net cash from operations (NCO), Capital expenditures (Capex).	NCO	CAPEX
Average for period	0.15	0.02
Dispersion	0.01	0.00

Main components of NCF relative to revenues, for each year:

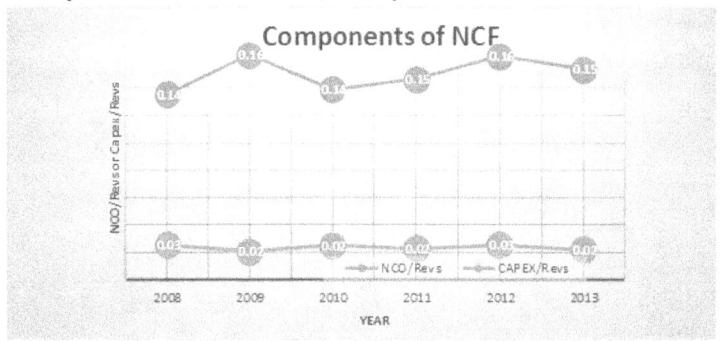

113

Note: *Business includes industrial machinery & components.*

***

61

TECHNOLOGY

Computer software: Prepackaged

Subsector   **Computer software: Prepackaged**
Most Recent FY   **2013 to Dec 31**
Observation Period: 6 years

Note: *Dispersion refers to the sample standard deviation, assuming normality. However the probability distribution may differ and the normal approximation may not be valid.*

1. CASH DIVIDEND GROWTH

Average growth over period	16.2%
Dispersion	41%

*Dividends are actual amounts reported.

Year-over-year dividend growth rates :

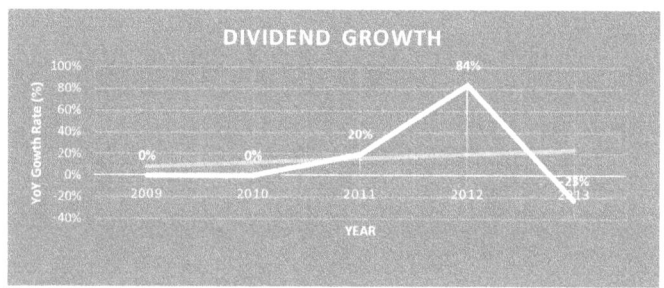

2. DIVIDEND COVERAGE RATIO

Average over period	3.76
Dispersion	0.94

Dividend coverage for each year:

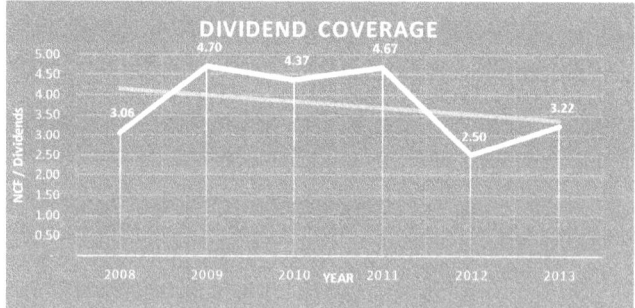

107

62

3. NET CASH FLOW (NCF) RATIO

Average over period	0.21
Dispersion	0.04

Net cash flow relative to revenues for each year:

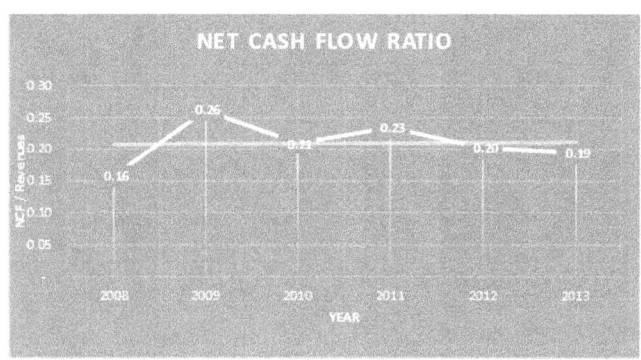

4. Components of NCF

Net cash from operations (NCO), Capital expenditures (Capex).	NCO	CAPEX
Average for period	0.24	0.03
Dispersion	0.03	0.00

Main components of NCF relative to revenues, for each year:

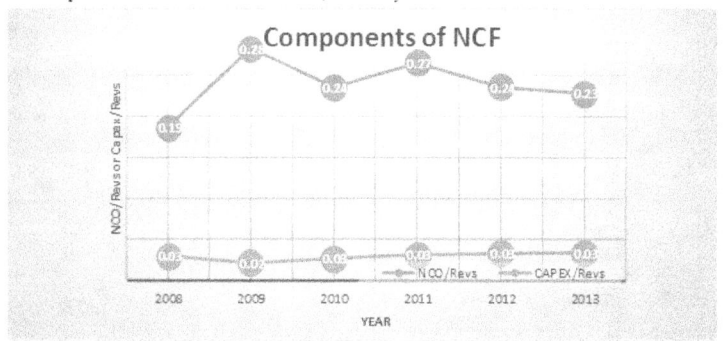

107

Subsector   **Computer software: Prepackaged**
Most Recent FY   **2014 to Jun 30**
Observation Period: 6 years
Note: *Dispersion refers to the sample standard deviation, assuming normality. However the probability distribution may differ and the normal approximation may not be valid.*

1. CASH DIVIDEND GROWTH

Average growth over period	14.9%
Dispersion	8%

*Dividends are actual amounts reported.

Year-over-year dividend growth rates :

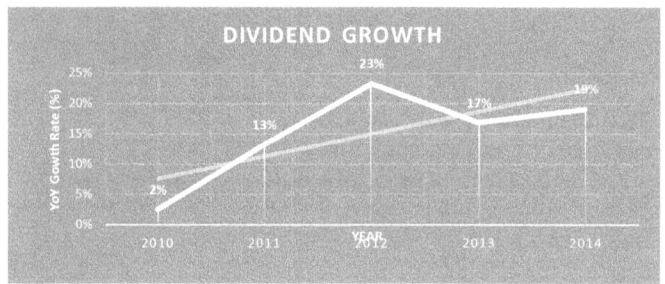

2. DIVIDEND COVERAGE RATIO

Average over period	4.01
Dispersion	0.81

Dividend coverage for each year:

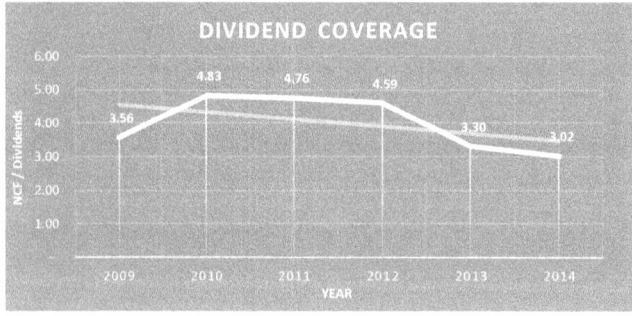

3. NET CASH FLOW (NCF) RATIO

Average over period	0.33
Dispersion	0.04

Net cash flow relative to revenues for each year:

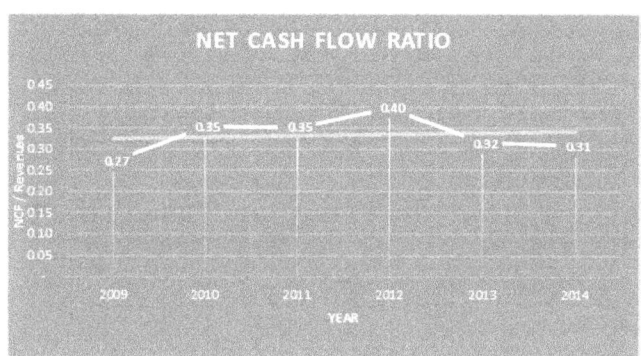

4. Components of NCF

Net cash from operations (NCO), Capital expenditures (Capex).	NCO	CAPEX
Average for period	0.38	0.04
Dispersion	0.03	0.01

Main components of NCF relative to revenues, for each year:

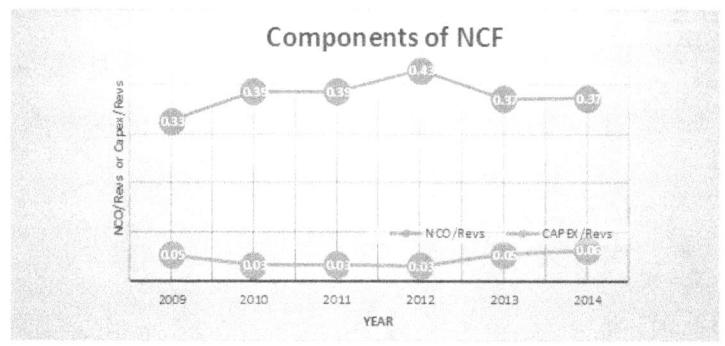

108

***

65

Computer software: Programming/Internet

Subsector	**Computer software: Programming/Internet**
Most Recent FY	**2013 to Dec 31**
Observation Period:	6 years

Note: *Dispersion refers to the sample standard deviation, assuming normality. However the probability distribution may differ and the normal approximation may not be valid.*

1. CASH DIVIDEND GROWTH

Average growth over period	#DIV/0!
Dispersion	#DIV/0!

*Dividends are actual amounts reported.

Year-over-year dividend growth rates :   Dividends were not paid during the period.

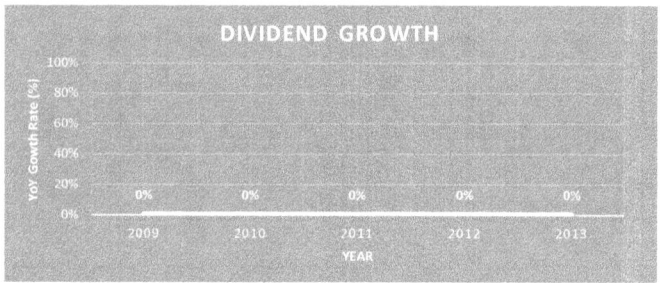

2. DIVIDEND COVERAGE RATIO

Average over period	#DIV/0!
Dispersion	#DIV/0!

Dividend coverage for each year:

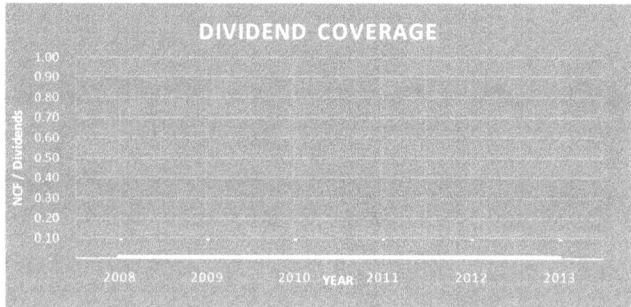

109

66

3. NET CASH FLOW (NCF) RATIO

Average over period	0.42
Dispersion	0.04

Net cash flow relative to revenues for each year:

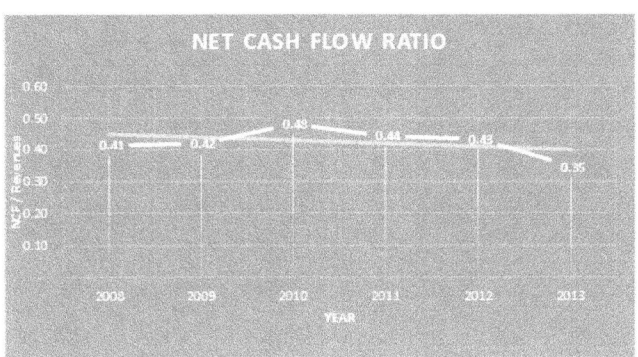

4. Components of NCF

Net cash from operations (NCO), Capital expenditures (Capex).	NCO	CAPEX
Average for period	0.53	0.11
Dispersion	0.06	0.02

Main components of NCF relative to revenues, for each year:

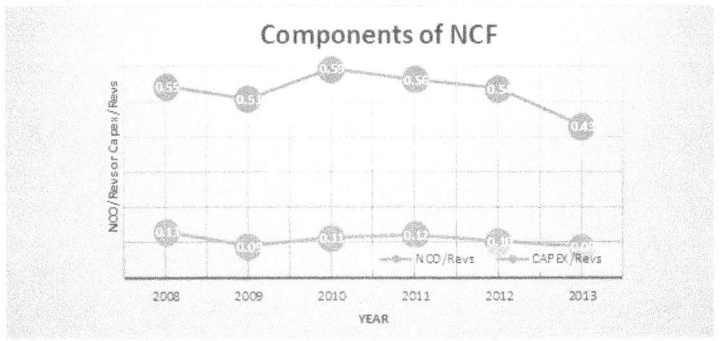

109

67

Subsector	Computer software: Programming/Internet
Most Recent FY	2013 to Dec 31
Observation Period:	6 years

Note: *Dispersion refers to the sample standard deviation, assuming normality. However the probability distribution may differ and the normal approximation may not be valid.*

1. CASH DIVIDEND GROWTH

Average growth over period	#DIV/0!
Dispersion	#DIV/0!

Dividends are actual amounts reported.

Year-over-year dividend growth rates : Dividends were not paid during the period.

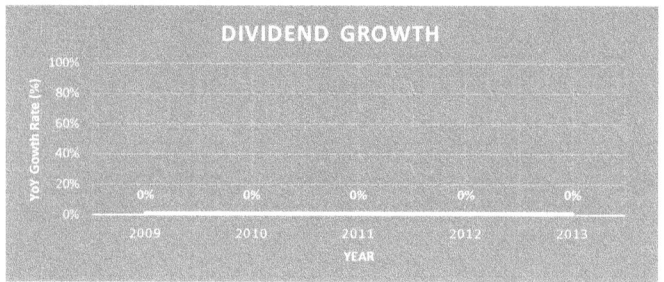

2. DIVIDEND COVERAGE RATIO

Average over period	#DIV/0!
Dispersion	#DIV/0!

Dividend coverage for each year:

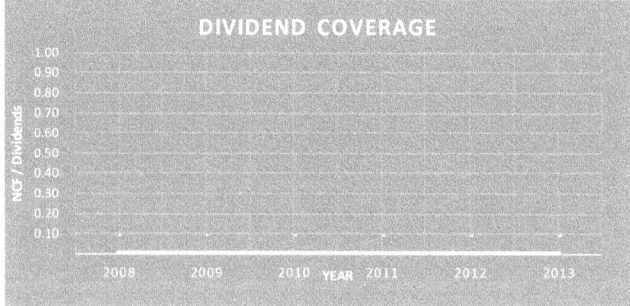

110

3. NET CASH FLOW (NCF) RATIO

Average over period	0.27
Dispersion	0.06

Net cash flow relative to revenues for each year:

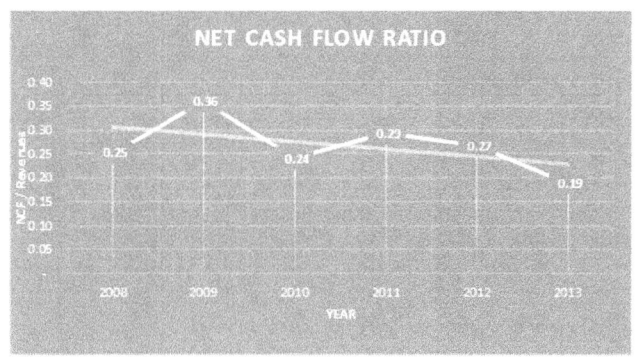

4. Components of NCF

Net cash from operations (NCO), Capital expenditures (Capex).	NCO	CAPEX
Average for period	0.36	0.09
Dispersion	0.03	0.04

Main components of NCF relative to revenues, for each year:

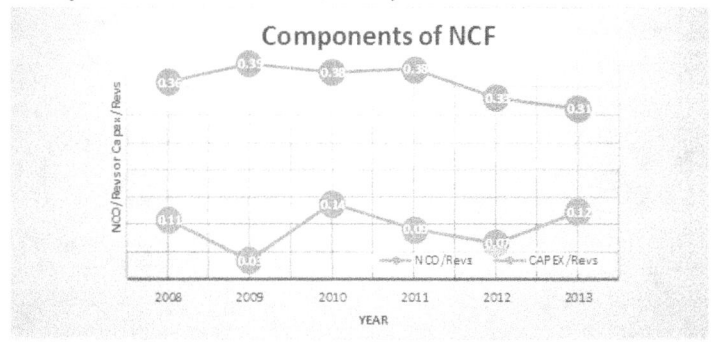

110

***

69

Technical & System Software

Subsector   Technical & system software
Most Recent FY   2014 to March 31
Observation Period: 6 years

Note: *Dispersion refers to the sample standard deviation, assuming normality. However the probability distribution may differ and the normal approximation may not be valid.*

1. CASH DIVIDEND GROWTH

Average growth over period	16.8%
Dispersion	87%

Dividends are actual amounts reported.

Year-over-year dividend growth rates :

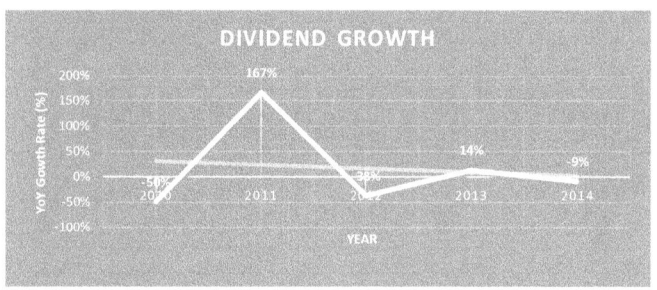

2. DIVIDEND COVERAGE RATIO

Average over period	3182.01
Dispersion	1129.28

Dividend coverage for each year:

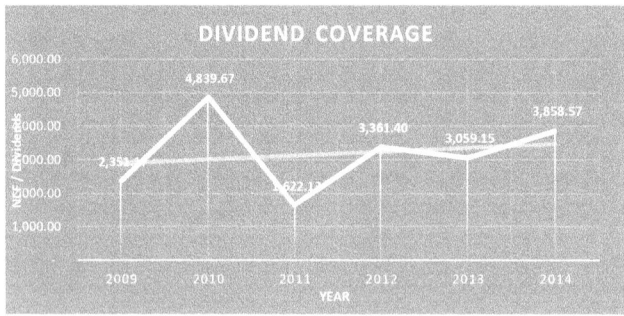

111

3. NET CASH FLOW (NCF) RATIO

Average over period	0.26
Dispersion	0.04

Net cash flow relative to revenues for each year:

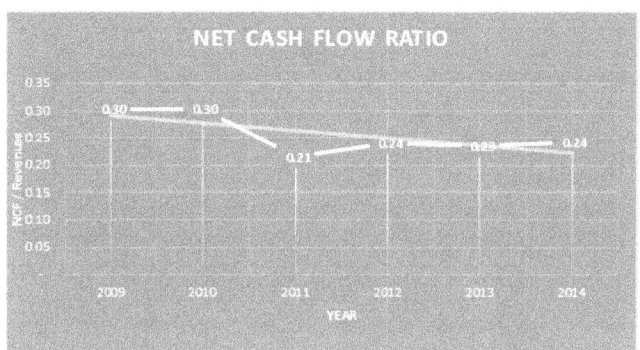

4. Components of NCF

Net cash from operations (NCO), Capital expenditures (Capex).	NCO	CAPEX
Average for period	0.26	0.00
Dispersion	0.04	0.00

Main components of NCF relative to revenues, for each year:

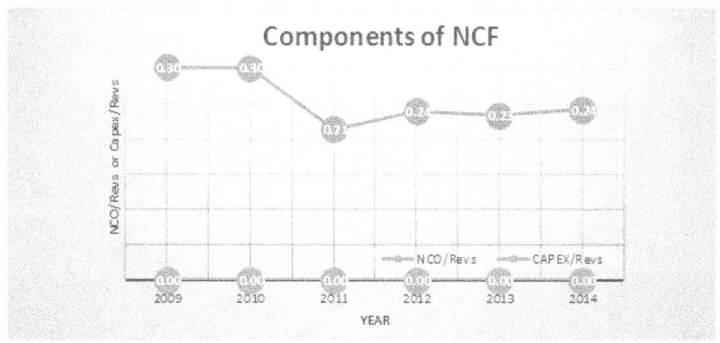

111

***

71

Communications Equipment

Subsector   **Communications equipment**
Most Recent FY   **2013 to Dec 31**
Observation Period: 6 years
Note: *Dispersion refers to the sample standard deviation, assuming normality. However the probability distribution may differ and the normal approximation may not be valid.*

1. CASH DIVIDEND GROWTH

Average growth over period	-33.3%
Dispersion	38%

*Dividends are actual amounts reported.
Year-over-year dividend growth rates :

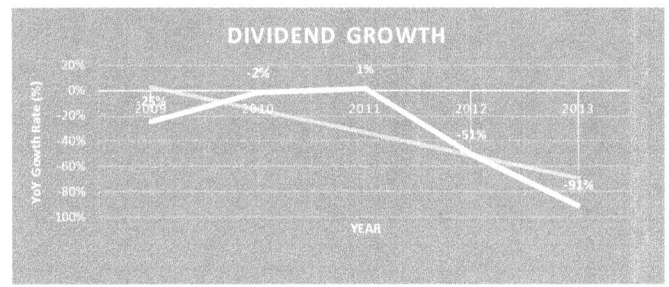

2. DIVIDEND COVERAGE RATIO

Average over period	0.02
Dispersion	2.65

Dividend coverage for each year:

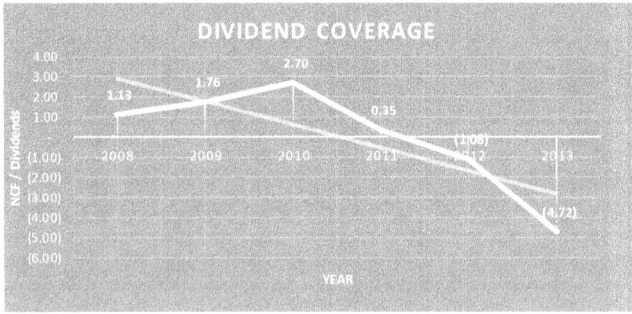

126

3. NET CASH FLOW (NCF) RATIO

Average over period	0.03
Dispersion	0.06

Net cash flow relative to revenues for each year:

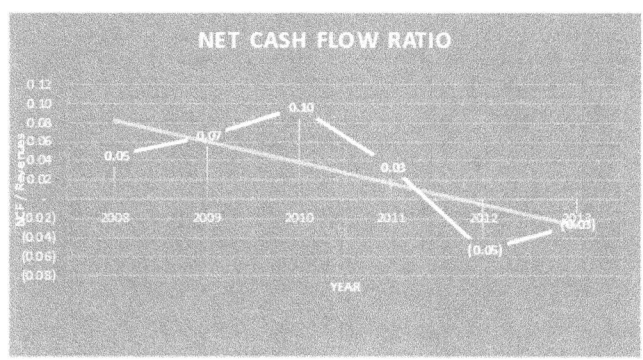

4. Components of NCF

Net cash from operations (NCO), Capital expenditures (Capex).	NCO	CAPEX
Average for period	0.06	0.02
Dispersion	0.04	0.01

Main components of NCF relative to revenues, for each year:

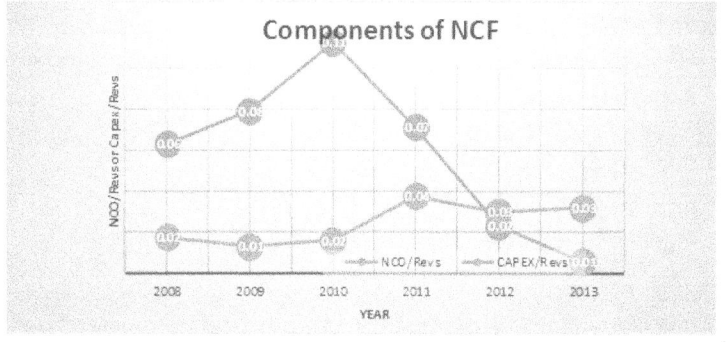

126

Note: *Data discrepancies may exist; 2008 revenue data unclear.*

Subsector	Communications equipment
Most Recent FY	2014 to Sep 28
Observation Period:	6 years

Note: *Dispersion refers to the sample standard deviation, assuming normality. However the probability distribution may differ and the normal approximation may not be valid.*

1. CASH DIVIDEND GROWTH

Average growth over period	19.1%
Dispersion	9%

*Dividends are actual amounts reported.

Year-over-year dividend growth rates :

2. DIVIDEND COVERAGE RATIO

Average over period	3.65
Dispersion	1.12

Dividend coverage for each year:

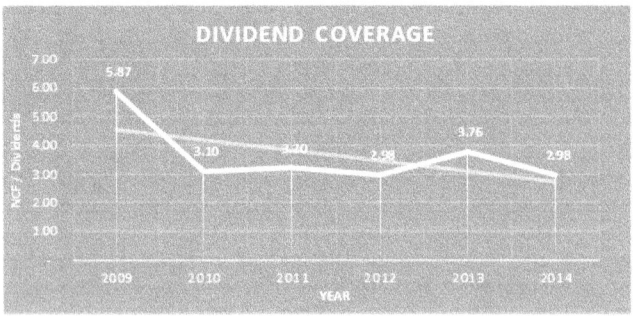

3. NET CASH FLOW (NCF) RATIO

Average over period	0.35
Dispersion	0.14

Net cash flow relative to revenues for each year:

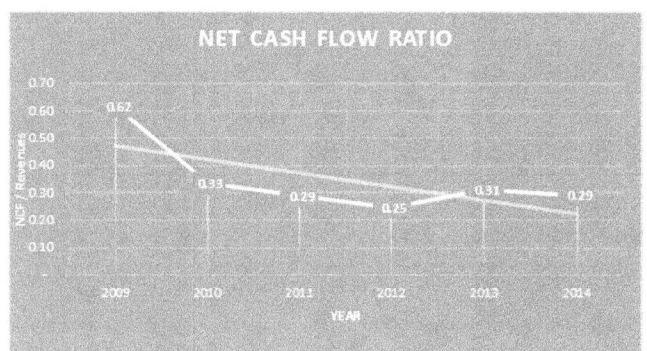

4. Components of NCF

Net cash from operations (NCO), Capital expenditures (Capex).	NCO	CAPEX
Average for period	0.40	0.05
Dispersion	0.14	0.02

Main components of NCF relative to revenues, for each year:

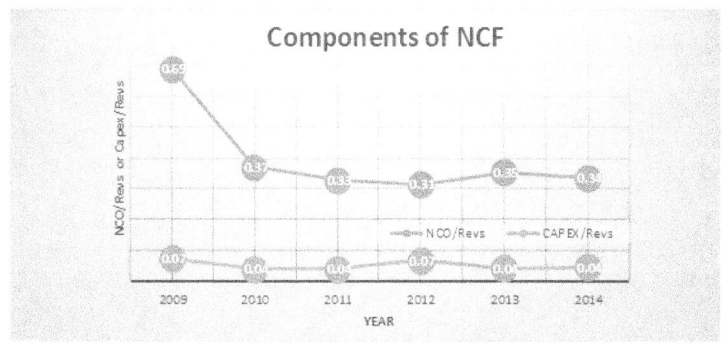

***

Semiconductor-Integrated Circuits

Subsector	Semiconductors
Most Recent FY	**2013 to Dec 31**
Observation Period:	6 years

Note: *Dispersion refers to the sample standard deviation, assuming normality. However the probability distribution may differ and the normal approximation may not be valid.*

1. CASH DIVIDEND GROWTH

Average growth over period	0.3%
Dispersion	0%

*Dividends are actual amounts reported.

Year-over-year dividend growth rates :

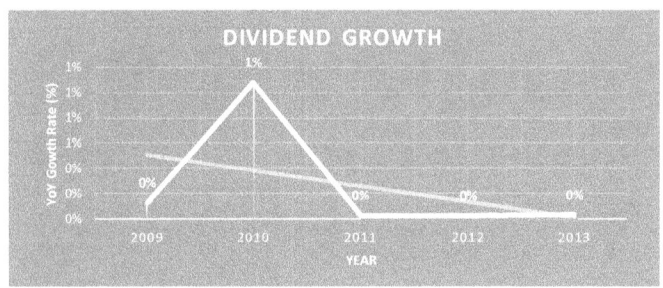

2. DIVIDEND COVERAGE RATIO

Average over period	0.88
Dispersion	0.63

Dividend coverage for each year:

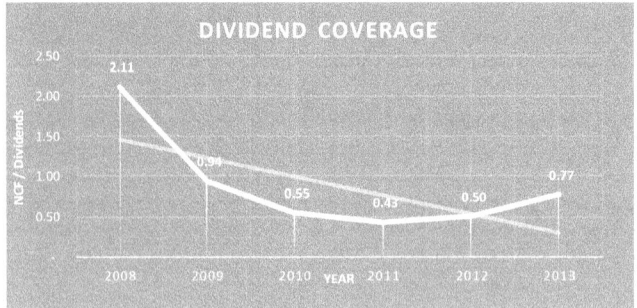

3. NET CASH FLOW (NCF) RATIO

Average over period	0.18
Dispersion	0.16

Net cash flow relative to revenues for each year:

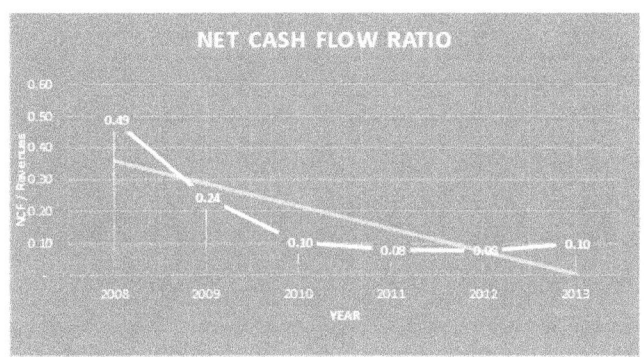

4. Components of NCF

Net cash from operations (NCO), Capital expenditures (Capex).	NCO	CAPEX
Average for period	0.58	0.40
Dispersion	0.05	0.13

Main components of NCF relative to revenues, for each year:

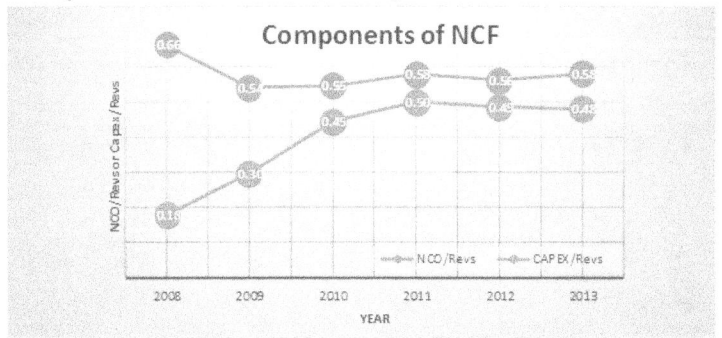

128

77

Semiconductor-Broad Line

Subsector   **Semiconductor-Broad Line**

Most Recent FY   **2013 to Dec 28**

Observation Period: 6 years

Note: *Dispersion refers to the sample standard deviation, assuming normality. However the probability distribution may differ and the normal approximation may not be valid.*

1. CASH DIVIDEND GROWTH

Average growth over period	7.8%
Dispersion	7%

*Dividends are actual amounts reported.

Year-over-year dividend growth rates :

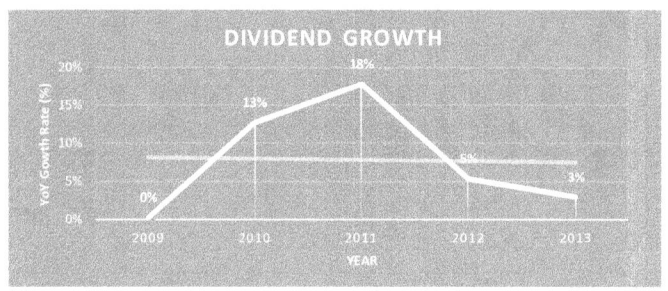

2. DIVIDEND COVERAGE RATIO

Average over period	2.30
Dispersion	0.54

Dividend coverage for each year:

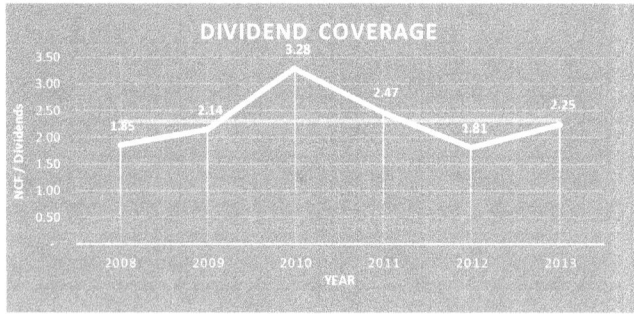

3. NET CASH FLOW (NCF) RATIO

Average over period	0.19
Dispersion	0.04

Net cash flow relative to revenues for each year:

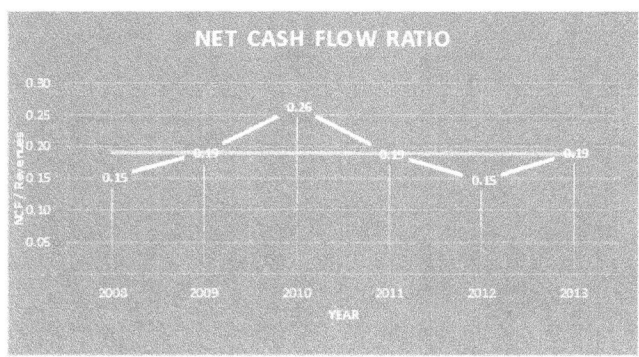

4. Components of NCF

Net cash from operations (NCO), Capital expenditures (Capex).

	NCO	CAPEX
Average for period	0.35	0.17
Dispersion	0.04	0.04

Main components of NCF relative to revenues, for each year:

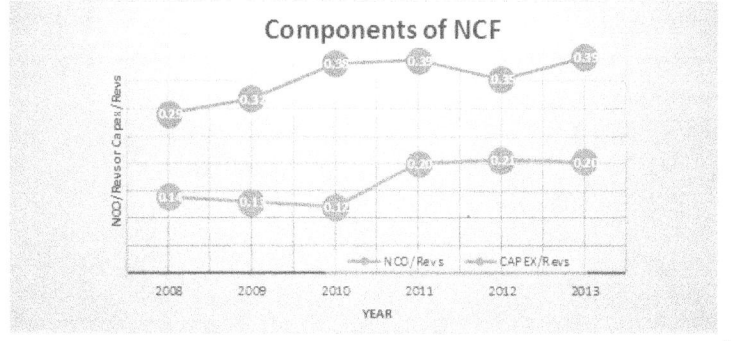

129

***

Telecommunications equipment

Subsector   **Telecommunications equipment**
Most Recent FY   **2013 Dec 31**
Observation Period: 6 years

Note: *Dispersion refers to the sample standard deviation, assuming normality. However the probability distribution may differ and the normal approximation may not be valid.*

1. CASH DIVIDEND GROWTH

Average growth over period	4.1%
Dispersion	3%

Dividends are actual amounts reported.

Year-over-year dividend growth rates :

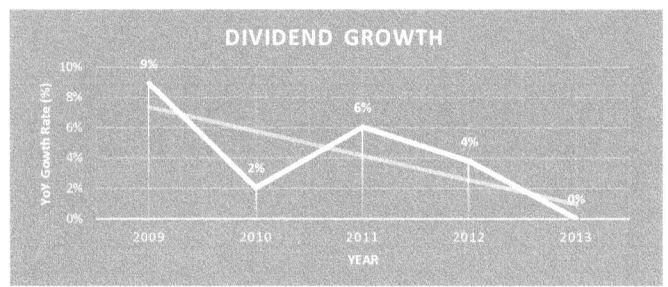

2. DIVIDEND COVERAGE RATIO

Average over period	1.89
Dispersion	0.29

Dividend coverage for each year:

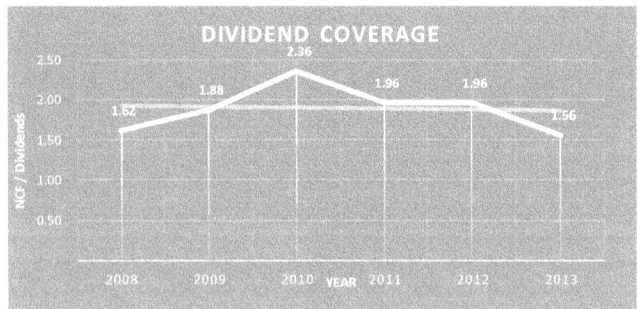

131

3. NET CASH FLOW (NCF) RATIO

Average over period	0.19
Dispersion	0.03

Net cash flow relative to revenues for each year:

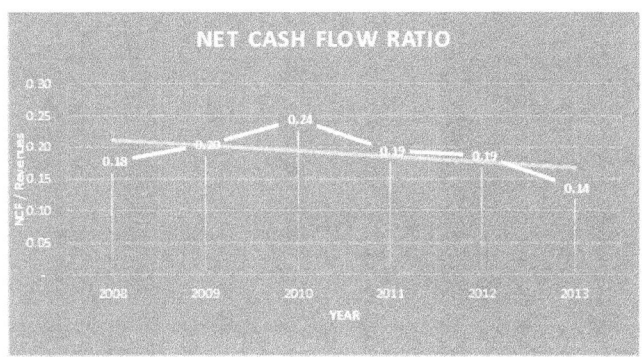

4. Components of NCF

Net cash from operations (NCO), Capital expenditures (Capex).	NCO	CAPEX
Average for period	0.43	0.24
Dispersion	0.05	0.03

Main components of NCF relative to revenues, for each year:

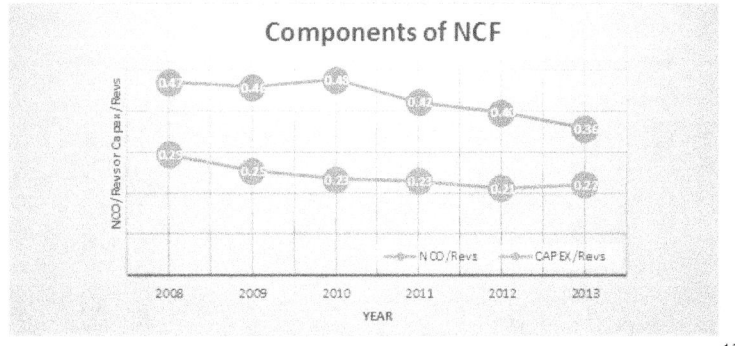

Subsector   **Telecommunications equipment**
Most Recent FY   **2013 to Dec 31**
Observation Period: 6 years

Note: *Dispersion refers to the sample standard deviation, assuming normality. However the probability distribution may differ and the normal approximation may not be valid.*

1. CASH DIVIDEND GROWTH

Average growth over period	0.4%
Dispersion	3%

*Dividends are actual amounts reported.

Year-over-year dividend growth rates :

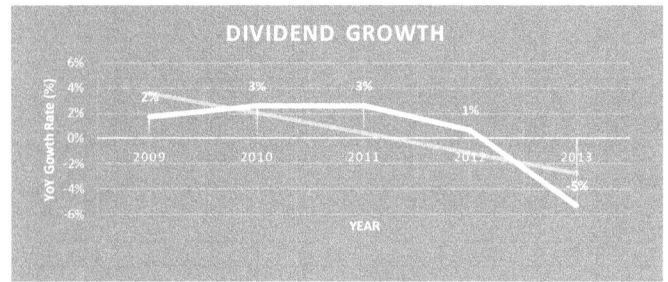

2. DIVIDEND COVERAGE RATIO

Average over period	1.57
Dispersion	0.22

Dividend coverage for each year:

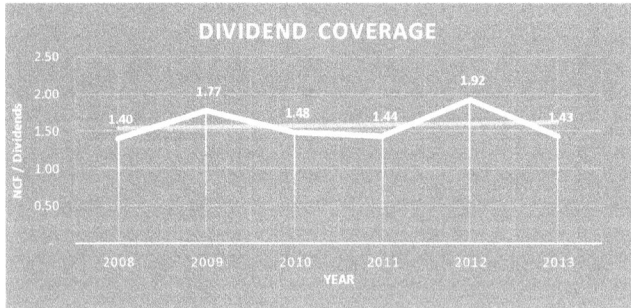

130

3. NET CASH FLOW (NCF) RATIO

Average over period	0.12
Dispersion	0.02

Net cash flow relative to revenues for each year:

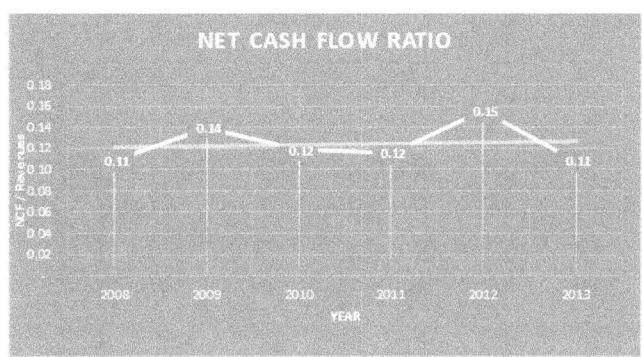

4. Components of NCF

Net cash from operations (NCO), Capital expenditures (Capex).	NCO	CAPEX
Average for period	0.28	0.16
Dispersion	0.01	0.01

Main components of NCF relative to revenues, for each year:

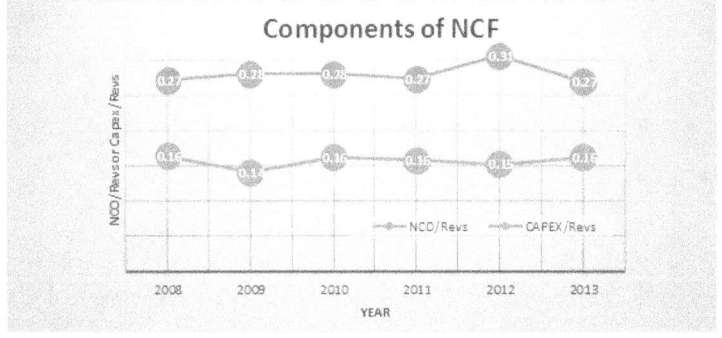

130

83

Subsector	Telecommunications equipment
Most Recent FY	**2013 to Dec 31**
Observation Period:	6 years

Note: *Dispersion refers to the sample standard deviation, assuming normality. However the probability distribution may differ and the normal approximation may not be valid.*

1. CASH DIVIDEND GROWTH

Average growth over period	34.3%
Dispersion	88%

*Dividends are actual amounts reported.

Year-over-year dividend growth rates :

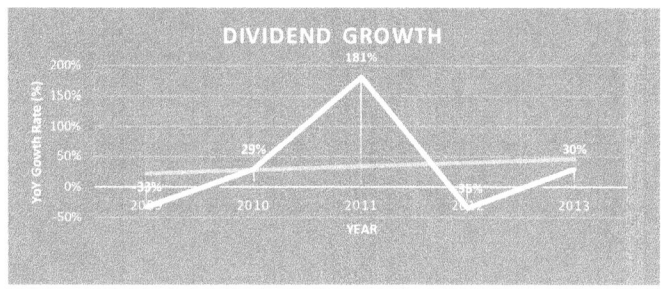

2. DIVIDEND COVERAGE RATIO

Average over period	1.18
Dispersion	0.36

Dividend coverage for each year:

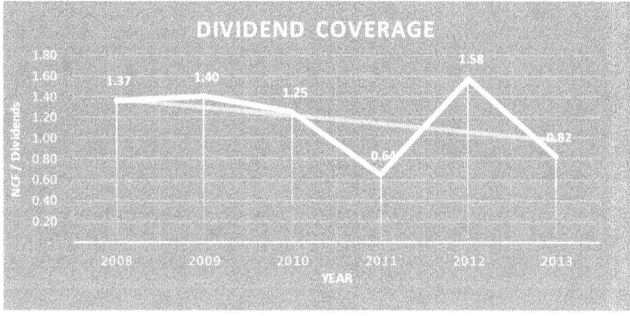

132

3. NET CASH FLOW (NCF) RATIO

Average over period	0.13
Dispersion	0.02

Net cash flow relative to revenues for each year:

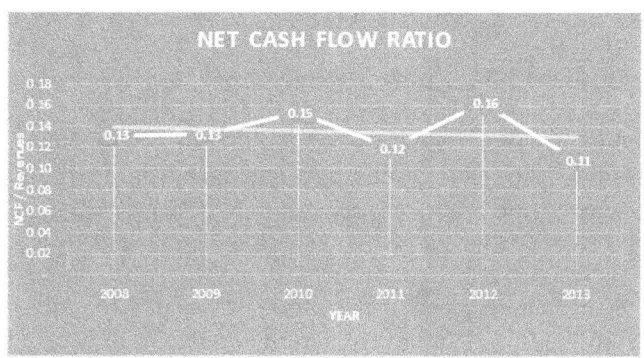

4. Components of NCF

Net cash from operations (NCO), Capital expenditures (Capex).	NCO	CAPEX
Average for period	0.27	0.14
Dispersion	0.03	0.03

Main components of NCF relative to revenues, for each year:

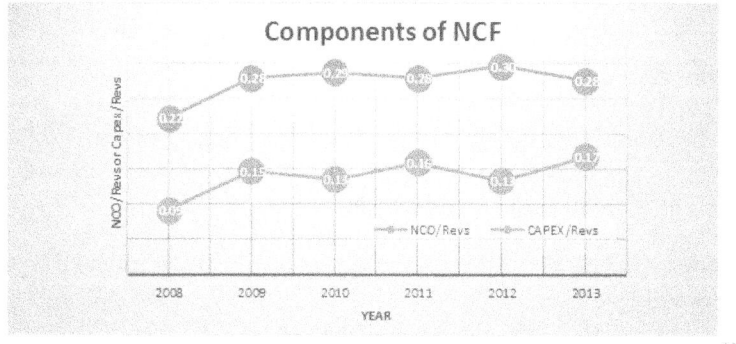

Note: *Financial statements were restated for FY 2012 and 2011.*

END OF REPORTS

APPENDICES

APPENDIX 1

Sample Data and Methodological Notes

The analytical framework above was applied to 32 non-financial firms, classified by sector, subsector and global in scope, with market capitalization totaling approximately US$3.8 trillion as of 2014.

Sample Selection. Non-financial firms were selected for this study. A primary objective was to diversify geographically. Where possible, two or more firms representing each subsector was also considered desirable for purposes of comparison. Quality of financial information was also viewed as fundamental. Firms listed on either the NYSE or the NASDAQ have audited financial statements and filings with the U.S. Securities and Exchange Commission (SEC). These filings are predominantly 20-F and 10-K reports.

The above criteria resulted in the sample excluding firms with less than $ U.S. 25B in market capitalization, as well as a concentration of sectors and subsectors.

Sectors. There are four sectors (*sector* is also often referred to as *industry*):
Basic materials (3 subsectors, 5 firms)
Consumer goods (6 subsectors, 9 firms)
Health care (3 subsectors*, 6 firms)
Technology (7 subsectors, 12 firms)

Subsectors. There are 19 or 20 subsectors depending on how certain firms are classified. Two firms in the health care category* have an industrial element that could classify them within the *industrial goods* sector as in two separate subsectors (*industrial machinery and components*, and *diversified machinery*). It was finally resolved to place these "hybrids" in the health care sector, under a single subsector titled "medical/industrial diversified."

Distribution of Firms and Sectors

Geographic. Firms are divided into four geographic regions: North America, Asia, Europe, and Other. North America consists of the United States (12 firms or 37.5% of the total), Canada and Mexico. Asia comprises firms from China, India and Japan. The "Other" category consists of firms from South Africa, Israel and Brazil. A total of 16 countries are represented (counting Hong Kong, Chinese Taipei/Taiwan and mainland China as a single unit). The country refers generally to the legal jurisdiction of incorporation, as reported to the SEC.

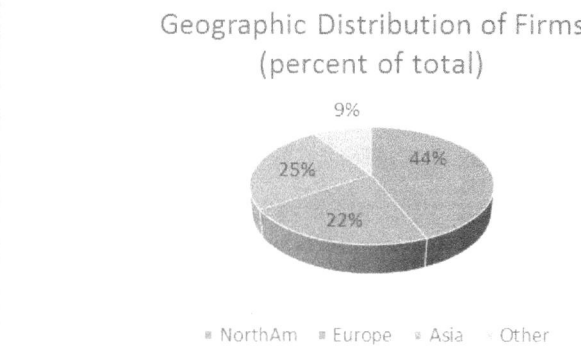

Geographic Distribution of Firms
(percent of total)

■ NorthAm ■ Europe ▪ Asia Other

Market Capitalization. The sample is heavily weighted in favor of the technology sector which comprises 49% of the total market capitalization. Within the technology sector, just 2 technology firms comprise 20% of the total market capitalization, both in the computer-software subsector, and both from the U.S.

Sector Distribution by Market Capitalization

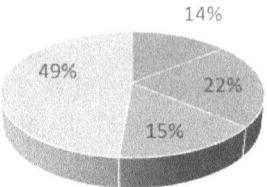

■ Basic Materials ■ Consumer Goods ■ Healthcare/Industrial ▪ Technology

Just 15 of the 32 firms represent 80% of the total market capitalization, of which 10 are from the U.S., 3 from China (including Chinese Taipei/Taiwan) and 2 from Europe (France and the Netherlands). Other important subsectors in terms of market capitalization include packaged goods/cosmetics (10% of the total market capitalization), telecommunications equipment (11%), oil & gas production-related (11%), and semiconductors (8%).

Firm Identification. Primary emphasis was placed on the sectors and subsectors in which the firms operate. This is in part due to the long-term likelihood of changes including mergers and acquisitions at which point certain names may be subsumed. Moreover, businesses can over time migrate from one subsector to another or straddle more than one subsector, as has been noted elsewhere. In addition, over time some subsectors may disappear in their current form in response to technological change, regulatory or other factors. Exchange-traded funds (ETFs) and mutual funds are popular vehicles to help investors diversify their holdings, and many of these have a sector focus. Grouping the data and estimates on the basis of sectors and subsectors may also be a useful reference in this regard.

Financial Data

Source. The data are sourced from the financial statements of the selected firms in either their filings with U.S. Securities and Exchange Commission (SEC), which are typically the 20-F or 10-K Reports, or company annual reports that include the financial statements.

The financial statements are generally audited by one of the "Big 4" accounting firms (formerly known as the "Big 8"), Deloitte Touche, Pricewaterhouse Coopers, Ernst&Young, and KPMG, sometimes possibly in conjunction with a local accounting office, whether or not affiliated with one of the four firms.

For non-U.S. dollar currencies, the currency units used are local and are not converted into U.S. dollars.

Observation Period. The sample data were collected from six fiscal years, referred to as the *observation period*. The fiscal years ranged from 2008 to 2013 (calendar year basis) for 23 of the firms, and from 2009 to 2014 for the remaining firms with fiscal years ending during 2014 (March, June and September).

Of particular interest is this observation period captures data from the financial crisis of 2008 forward, and may offer insight into world economic conditions from the perspective of sectors, subsectors and individual firms within the sample.

Fiscal Year. Most firms report their financial information on a *calendar-year basis* i.e. for one year ending on December 31 of that year. For firms that report their financial information on another basis, the fiscal year is generally advanced by one year. For example, if ABC Inc.'s fiscal year ends on December 31st, 2013, the fiscal year is calendar year basis and is referred to as fiscal year 2013 (or abbreviated as FY 2013). If XYZ, Inc.'s fiscal year ends June 30th, 2014, XYZ's fiscal year is referred to as FY 2014.

Data Series. The data from each year of the observation period are grouped into four original series: Revenues, net cash from operations, capital expenditures, and dividends. Since each data observation corresponds to a fiscal year, for an observation period of six fiscal years the sample size of each series is six; it is recognized that the sample size is very small.

A fifth series, *net cash flow* (also referred to as net free cash flow or *free cash flow* and abbreviated NCF as noted previously) is constructed by subtracting capital expenditures from net cash from operations for each fiscal year. This measure and shortcomings are discussed at length in the framework section.

Financial Metrics. These five series are used to construct financial metrics, each corresponding to a section in the reports: Cash Dividend Growth Rate, Dividend Coverage Ratio, Net Cash flow Ratio, and Components of NCF. Each metric is discussed in in the section on reading the reports.

The question may arise as to why common metrics such as the *dividend yield* or *dividend payout ratio* are not shown in the analysis.

The dividend yield is acknowledged as important, but is considered to be less indicative of the capacity of the firm to generate equity income for investors. Share prices can fluctuate considerably and may or may not reflect a company's underlying financial strength. The dividend paid per share does not necessarily provide underlying information about the firm's equity income generating capacity, and can vary according to the number of shares outstanding. A cash dividend growth rate measure is provided here but is based upon the actual dividend amounts paid.

The dividend payout ratio is typically computed by dividing dividends by net income. The dividend coverage ratio used in this analysis is net cash flow (NCF) divided by dividends. As discussed in the framework section, because NCF is regarded as the *primary source of payment* for dividends, NCF is preferred to net income. An alternative dividend payout ratio using NCF can be derived by taking the reciprocal of the dividend coverage ratio as presented herein. Note however that the dividend coverage ratio itself has shortcomings that are discussed in the framework section and in possible extensions to the analysis.

Data Discrepancies. The terminology and composition of data may differ somewhat across firms. The data series are assumed to be reasonably uniform but not identical in all cases.

Although the financial information is considered to be of good quality, certain data discrepancies were found that could not be satisfactorily reconciled, and are noted. Some financial statements were restated in subsequent years.

In certain cases, the composition of capital expenditures was not clarified. Inclusion of capitalized interest, capitalized exploration expenditures or intangibles may depend on firm reporting practices. Figures for net cash from operations were in a few cases inconsistently reported, and an arbitrary decision had to be made to select the most appropriate data for the sample.

Financial statements may be restated in subsequent years. The data used are subject to revisions and may be updated from time to time.

APPENDIX 2

Estimates from Earlier Data Sets and Normality Testing

This appendix summarizes an informal analysis of a sample of 173 observations taken from annual financial data of non-financial public companies from fiscal years 1988 to 2001.

NCF Ratio Estimates. Sample sizes for the individual firm data within the observation period were very small (10 or less observations per firm). Eleven firms were selected from the basic materials, consumer goods and technology sectors. The average and sample standard deviation of each firm selected was computed for the NCF ratio (NCF/Revenues) for the fiscal years 1988 to 2001.

The combined average of the estimates for the 11 firms was 0.101 for the average and 0.052 for the sample standard deviation. For the last five fiscal years of the sample, 1997 to 2001, the combined average of the estimates were 0.099 and 0.054, respectively.

Sector average and sample standard deviations were as follows:
Basic Materials: 0.044, 0.008.
Consumer Goods: 0.042, 0.014.
Technology: 0.203, 0.025.

Normality testing was conducted on the ratio of net cash from operations to revenues (NCO/Revenues) on the 173 observations. The average of the NCO/Revenue ratio was 0.15 with a standard deviation of 0.11. The evidence from normality testing suggested that the population was not normally distributed. The computed chi-square value of 9.97 fell outside of the acceptance region for most levels of significance (alpha) with a probability of less than 2% that the population was normally distributed. These normality results should in no way be regarded as valid or conclusive. However, the possibility that certain financial measures may not be normally distributed should be given consideration. Clarifying the underlying probability distributions can be instructive not only in equity income analysis, but can also help evaluate debt service capacity and default probabilities in credit analysis.

***

www.ingramcontent.com/pod-product-compliance
Lightning Source LLC
Chambersburg PA
CBHW070828180526
45168CB00002B/772